THE DARWEN COUNTY
HISTORY SERIES

A History of
SUSSEX

The Royal Pavilion, Brighton, in 1821. Plans for extending the building and transforming it were drawn up first by Repton and finally by John Nash. The exterior design was much influenced by Indian architecture. With the death of George IV in 1830 Brighton ceased to be the favourite resort of the monarchy.

THE DARWEN COUNTY HISTORY SERIES

A History of
SUSSEX

J.R. Armstrong

edited by
Richard Pailthorpe and Diana Zeuner

Phillimore

1995

Published by
PHILLIMORE & CO. LTD.
Shopwyke Manor Barn, Chichester, West Sussex

First published 1961
Fourth edition 1995

© Weald and Downland Museum, 1995

ISBN 0 85033 946 4

Printed and bound in Great Britain by
BUTLER AND TANNER LTD.
Frome, Somerset

Contents

List of Illustrations

Frontispiece: The Royal Pavilion, Brighton, in 1821

List of Colour Illustrations

Preface

Roy Armstrong devoted his life to concern for history, particularly local history and especially the way in which ordinary people have lived. His *History of Sussex*, first published in 1961 and revised by him in 1978, remains one of the primary history books on the county. One year after his death, we were therefore honoured to be approached by Phillimore to edit a revised edition for the 1990s.

Before we had completed the task we were saddened by the death of his wife Lyn, who had been pleased that it was to be undertaken by two people connected closely with Roy Armstrong's greatest achievement, the Weald and Downland Open Air Museum at Singleton, West Sussex.

The Museum embodied many of the values Roy held dearest. Deeply concerned about the vanishing vernacular achitecture of the south east, he aimed to preserve some of the best examples of local traditional buildings and interpret to visitors the way of life led by their occupants. The Museum was built on voluntary determination and effort, inspired by Roy's leadership, and remains so today. Twenty years after its foundation the achievement of its main objective is evident—the recognition of the importance of these buildings to history and the value of their preservation on their original sites. Historic buildings are no longer being demolished wholesale—people care for them and new uses are being sought. Roy also played his part in the conservation of the natural heritage through the Sandgate Preservation Society which he founded near his home in Storrington to preserve 1,000 acres of threatened landscape.

Roy's major revision of the book incorporated more information on buildings than the first edition. In this edition we have tried to integrate further this information within the chapters, thus bringing together the way in which ordinary people lived with the other events and aspects of Sussex history.

We have also taken the opportunity of bringing up to date the many important archaeological discoveries made in the county over the last two decades; and introduced a new chapter, 'Twentieth-Century Sussex', incorporating aspects of the economy and social life of our recent times, particularly the conservation of the county's heritage in all its variety. In doing this we would like to acknowledge most gratefully the help of people who have been closely involved with these developments.

Finally we wish to dedicate this edition to its author Roy Armstrong and his wife Lyn, who between them achieved so much for conservation in the county and whose work has enriched the lives of all of us living in Sussex today.

RICHARD PAILTHORPE and DIANA ZEUNER

Acknowledgements

The editors would like to thank the many people and organisations who have helped in the editing of this book by advising, lending photographs, providing information and assisting with editing. We are most grateful to the following for their generous assistance: Alec Down; David Rudkin, Director, Fishbourne Roman Palace; Richard Harris, Research Director, Weald and Downland Open Air Museum; Mark Taylor, County Archaeologist, West Sussex County Council; John Godfrey, Assistant County Secretary, West Sussex County Council and members of the County Council staff; R.Partridge, Assistant County Secretary, East Sussex County Council and members of the County Council staff; D. Beevers, Brighton Museum and Art Gallery; Dr. S.White, Worthing Museum and Art Gallery; the Port of Shoreham Authority; Newhaven Port Authority; Ministry of Agriculture; The Forestry Authority; Sussex Downs Conservation Board; The Wey & Arun Canal Trust; The Wildlife and Wetlands Trust; The Sussex Federation of Amenity Societies; The Sussex Industrial Archaeology Society; The Sussex Wildlife Trust; M. Sorrell; D. Rudling, Director, South Eastern Archaeological Services.

The following pictures and illustrations have been taken from the original text and credited to: Crown Copyright Reserved, 11; Phaidon Press Ltd., London, 41, 42 (The Bayeux Tapestry by Sir Frank Stenton); Noel Habgood, F.R.P.S., 78; Worthing Public Library, 108, 109, 137; British Museum, 97; J.K. St Joseph (Cambridge University Copyright), 45; J.R. Armstrong, V, 82.

The editors are most grateful to the following for the loan of photographs and illustrations: Arundel Museum & Heritage Centre, 110; Brighton Museum and Art Gallery, 130; *Chichester Observer*, XIV; P. Drewett, 14; J. Dallaway, *History of West Sussex*, 47; Peter Dunn, courtesy of English Heritage, 5; D.R. Elleray, 147, 149; Fishbourne Roman Palace (Sussex Archaeological Society), 25, 26; Gatwick Airport Ltd., XVI; Richard Harris, 81, 128; Alan Sorrell (Worthing Museum and Art Gallery photograph), 46; I. Serraillier, 131, 133, 139-41; J. Symons, frontispiece; Tangmere Military Aviation Museum, 155; Weald and Downland Open Air Museum, XIII, 90, 119, 121, 164; West Sussex County Record Offi ce (Kim Leslie/David Nicholls), 69 (George Garland Collection), 122; West Sussex County Council, 89; *West Sussex Gazette*, 53. The remaining photographs have been taken by R. Pailthorpe.

Our thanks to Graham Butler for drawings and cartography, 10, 132, 134, 159, 165. Cartography from the original edition by J. Broughton and Roy Mole, and drawings by Caroline Lockwood.

1

The Geographical Setting

An imaginary traveller with no particular objective in view, finding himself in the centre of the Sussex Weald at some point not too far from Wych Cross or Turner's Hill, might look to the north or to the south, wondering which direction to take. From one point of view it would make little difference. In both cases he would find himself walking for some miles through steep wooded valleys, with many streams and prosperous farms, built of half timber or local yellow-brown stone, and small fields of rich pasture and ploughland—sometimes across sandy heathland plateaux, with little but pine and birch and bracken, where he might chance on a low outcrop of weathered sandstone.

1 *Oast house, High Weald*

After five or six miles he would gradually descend to a low wooded plain. Here the oak is characteristic, the remains of a dense oak forest, which for some two thousand years covered the wealden clay. The farms are oak-framed and often roofed with a large, heavy, grey-brown, moss encrusted sandstone tile, the fields often separated or edged by dense oak and hazel coppices. After six or seven miles through the rutted, sticky ways of this weald clay, he would approach a series of low hills of a quite different kind, rising in places to two or three hundred feet. Here are many small villages rather close together with a landscape not unlike that from which he started—light sandy soils and stretches of heavier loam, with the older buildings mainly of a grey-brown local sandstone.

Finally, after crossing another narrow plain of heavy clay almost devoid of buildings, he would find himself facing the steep escarpment of the chalk Downs. Here he would enter a region very different in its trees, flowers and wild life, and in the character and size of its farms. Strung along the slightly raised shelf below the escarpment are many farms and small hamlets. The buildings are mainly of flint or a whitish-grey stone called Malm stone, which outcrops just below the chalk. Climbing to the top of the Downs he would see the chalk hills sloping gradually away. From the North Downs, London and the Thames valley would lie on the horizon; from the South Downs, the coastal plain of Sussex and the English Channel.

2 *Flint mine, Downland Area*

Today these southern slopes of the Downs are amongst the least populated parts of Sussex, an area of large farms and few villages. Traditional structures, from churches to garden walls, are of flint, and many villages preserve something of the unique quality they possessed a century ago. These downland slopes, now partly ploughed, were, less than a generation ago, open sheep pastures, and had been so for six centuries or more. Before that they were abandoned scrubland; before that an area of small cultivated fields, cattle enclosures, and hilltop towns; still earlier a region of scattered flint mines, settlements of miners and flint tool makers; before this the main highway between the upland farms and causewayed camps of colonists from the west. Climate played its part in some of these changes, invasion and the introduction of new farming techniques in others, and in the middle of this century an economy determined by war or the threat of war. Changes such as these form the basis of local history.

Assuming our traveller has climbed the Downs somewhere between Ditchling Beacon and Chanctonbury Ring, he will, to the south-west, see the flat coastal plain widening gradually until, at Chichester, it is over ten miles across, whilst to the south-east the chalk formation reaches to the sea, and forms an undulating sequence of valley and cliff, terminating at Beachy Head. Some of the richest farmland in Sussex is found in the coastal plain,

3 *The setting*

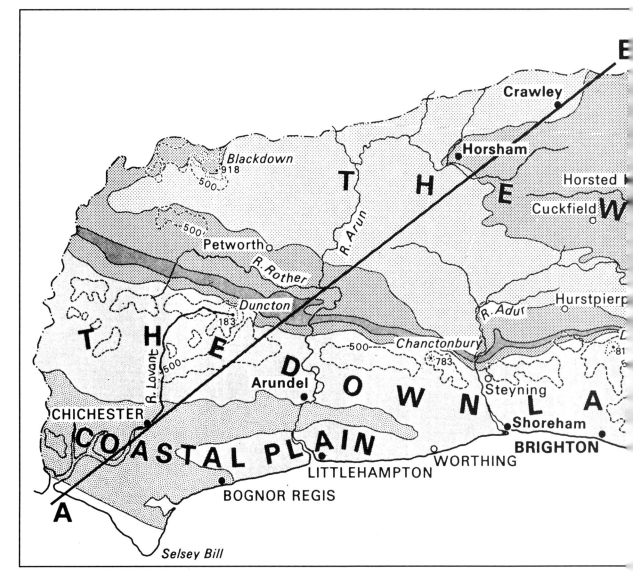

which for the last two thousand years has been the most populated area. Here again our traveller will find, generally, the same mixed clays, sands and gravels as he would, had he travelled north and descended into the Thames valley. If a line is drawn from Hastings along the ridges of the central Weald, through Crowborough and Hand Cross to Horsham, the landscape on either side of this line is rather like a mirror image of that on the other side. It is this basic symmetry which makes Sussex and the wealden landscape a fascinating area to geologists and geographers. A clear picture of these varied and roughly parallel regions is fundamental to an understanding of Sussex, especially of the changes and sequence of human settlement there.

There is however one feature which the traveller, however observant, will not realise. The coast line with its bays and estuaries, shingle bars and promontories, which appear so defined and stable, has in fact been and still is in a condition of continuous flux. This is due to a number of causes—

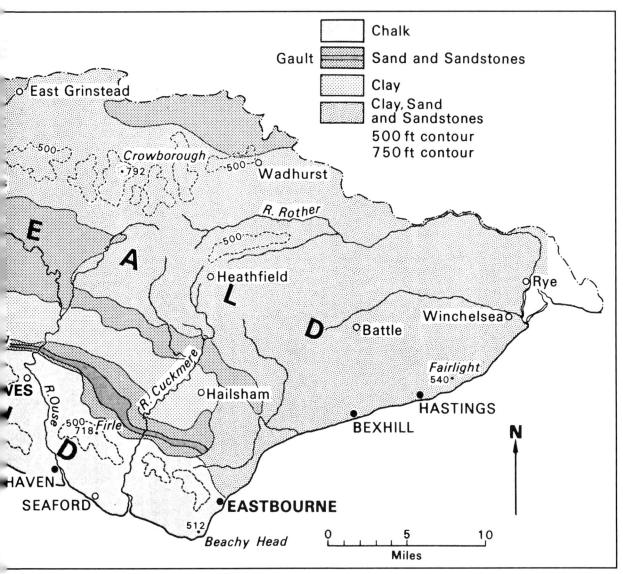

4 *The Weald is a landscape of small pasture fields with hedges and woodland. This view from Firle Beacon looks across the Low Weald, a low-lying clay vale surrounding the central sandstone upland of the High Weald.*

erosion by the sea, the silting of estuaries and rivers, and at times the slow but gradual alteration in the level of sea or land. These changes, slow in terms of the lifetime of the individual but rapid in the wider context of history, have had an incalculable effect on trade, the rise and decline of ports and market centres, and on the distribution and movement of population.

In Neolithic times, some four to five thousand years ago, the coastal plain must have extended several miles further to the south. Since then the rate of erosion has been most continuous at the western end of the county, where the great flat triangle of the Manhood peninsula extends from Chichester to Selsey. Here, even in Roman times, land stretched perhaps three miles further to the sea than it does today, and the denudation still continues. Here, engulfed by the sea, lie Belgic as well as Saxon towns and settlements.

At the other end of the county the process has been reversed. Southwesterly storms and currents have carried debris from the west to build shingle bars and sand banks across the river estuaries to the east, blocking harbours and accelerating the silting up of river valleys. Pevensey, Winchelsea and Rye, once great sea ports, now lie stranded miles from the present coast, while safe and adequate harbours such as once existed at Fishbourne, Steyning (St Cuthman's port), Old Shoreham, Meeching, Bulverhythe and Hastings have been so long completely silted up that they are now built over and virtually unidentifiable.

2

The First Inhabitants

With the onset of the last Ice Age, during which the ice sheets crept as far south as the northern sides of the Thames valley, subarctic conditions drove these people far to the south. Evidence of the first living person to be found in Sussex, and at that time, in Europe, dates back to the lower Paleolithic period. In 1994 a discovery of international importance was made in a gravel pit at Boxgrove, near Chichester, when archaeologists discovered a shin bone, which was dated as 500,000 years old. The tibia belonged to a species called Homo Heidebergensis. 'Boxgrove Man', as its owner became known, was probably about twenty years old at the time of his death, more than six feet tall and weighed more than twelve stone. The climate at this time would have been temperate and the site is on the edge of what was once the Goodwood-Slindon raised beach, rising some hundred feet above the present sea level. The beach possibly extended from Portsdown in Hampshire to the River Arun. Tools would have been made from flint worked from the cliff face and used for butchering animals. The remains of a horse, whose bones had been broken up to extract marrow for nourishment, were made. Evidence reveals that these people's diet included rhinoceros, red deer and bear. Futher archaeological excavation in 1995 revealed a human tooth dating from several hundred years earlier than the shinbone. Ten thousand years ago, however, conditions had so far improved with the retreat of the ice sheet again, that hunters following game from the east crossed what is now the North Sea, but which was then dry land, to Britain. They moved from one temporary encampment to another in various parts of England, including a number in Sussex. These people we can definitely think of as our own remote ancestors, but like the earlier Palaeolithic hunters they were still nomadic, and did not practise agriculture. They made delicately fashioned arrow- and spearheads, and carved bone harpoons and fish-hooks, and for some five or six thousand years hunted animals such as the auroch. Very large numbers of their knives, scrapers, arrow-heads and other tools have been found in Sussex. Notable sites are those at Westhampnett near Chichester, Chithurst and West Heath in the western Rother valley, near Midhurst, and at Selmeston near Firle. At Selmeston one pit yielded over 6,400 worked flints.

During this period, which is known as the Mesolithic Age, the ice sheets over Scandinavia and the North were melting rapidly, and gradually raised the levels of seas and oceans—whereas during the onset of the last Ice Age,

5   *Boxgrove Man*

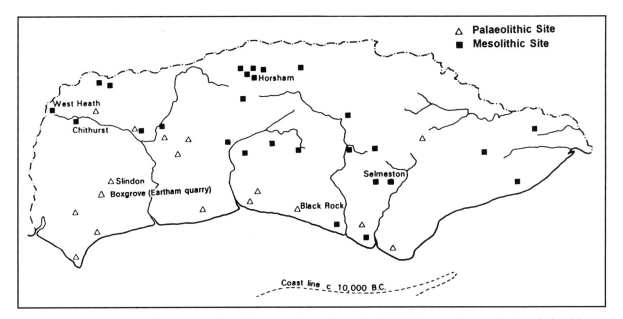

△ **Palaeolithic Site**
■ **Mesolithic Site**

Horsham

West Heath △

Chithurst △

△ Slindon
△ Boxgrove (Eartham quarry)

Selmeston

△ Black Rock

Coast line c 10,000 B.C.

6 *Palaeolithic and* the sea level had dropped until the British Isles, and even Iceland, had been
Mesolithic Sussex linked to the Continent by the drained land. At the beginning of the
Mesolithic period, therefore, there was no division between Sussex and
Northern France, only a rather flat plain with a river flowing down the
centre of what is now the English Channel. Gradually this river widened
from the west, and the estuary where it entered the sea encroached further
and further to the east. We must imagine those Mesolithic groups, who
possibly migrated from north to south following the seasons, having to
make, over the centuries, a longer and longer detour to the east when
crossing this river. At some point, possibly about seven or eight thousand
years ago, the estuary had reached as far as Dover, and there must have
been some dramatic event—the result of storm and high tides—when the
encroaching sea from the north joined the widening channel from the east,
thus forming the Straits of Dover. Once this breach had taken place, the
rapid flow of tides and the effect of rough weather would quickly widen the
strait, cutting off the Mesolithic people of the Weald from the Continent.

7 *Palaeolithic imple-* Perhaps for two or three thousand years there was little or no contact and
ment, Slindon during this time the English Channel and the Sussex coastline slowly
approached their present form.

Towards the middle of the third millennium B.C. the first true invasion
and colonisation occurred. Peoples, originally from the Mediterranean, landed
first in Ireland and the south-west of England, and then pushed eastward
along the hills and chalk plateaux of the south. These wiry dark-haired
people possessed the basic crafts of civilisation—pottery, weaving, agriculture
and the domestication of animals. They were very different from the nomadic
hunters of the Weald and were capable of a highly organised social life;
witness the great temples erected at Avebury in Wiltshire, and later at
Stonehenge. Though the centre of this 'Neolithic' civilisation was on the

chalk hills of the Salisbury Plain area, it spread along the Downs. Of the 12 hill-top settlements or 'causewayed camps' built by these Neolithic people in the south of England, four are in Sussex. These are at Whitehawk above Brighton, on the Trundle north of Chichester, at Barkhale above Bignor, and on Coombe Hill above Eastbourne. They are called 'causewayed' because the surrounding banks and ditches are broken by undefended gaps. Two of these 'camps' (the Trundle and Whitehawk) have been partly excavated, and some light has been shed on the life of the communities. Important burials were in long mounds or 'barrows' and, of these, seven have been found in Sussex; one, called Bevis's Thumb, near the summit of the Downs at North Marden, measures approximately 150 feet in length by over twenty in breadth.

8 *Neolithic vessel, Cissbury*

Perhaps the most interesting feature of this Neolithic culture in Sussex is the mining of flints for implement making. These mines are all located on the upper chalk strata, the only part of the chalk containing flint in any quantity. Not only was this known, but it was also known where the most suitable form of flint was likely to be found. Flint mine-shafts are found fairly close together. On Cissbury Down above Worthing there are over 150 within a radius of a few hundred yards. They are usually fifteen to twenty feet deep and about the same in width.

It seems probable that the Neolithic invasion of Southern Britain was stimulated by a rapid improvement in the climate, and there is evidence that for a time it may have been both warmer and wetter than it is today. The Neolithic settlements seem to have been concentrated on the Downs, where many of the now dry valleys may then have contained springs. A relatively small change in the prevailing wind currents or in the course of the Gulf Stream could cause dramatic changes in our climate. Major alterations in

9 *Neolithic and Bronze-Age Sussex*

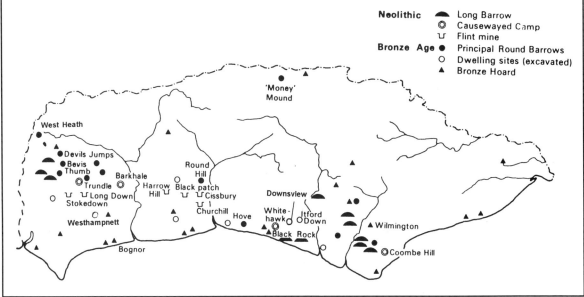

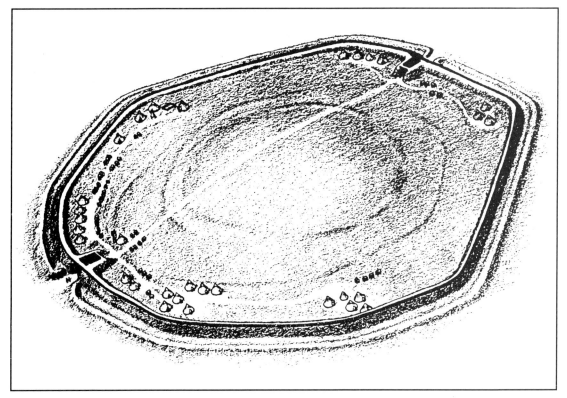

10 *The Trundle was first occupied during the Neolithic period (5000-4000 B.C.) defended by a series of concentric ditches. The Iron-Age hill fort dates from the 4th century B.C. and was probably abandoned in about 100 B.C.*

11 *Cissbury looking north east. The width across the Iron-Age enclosure is approximately 1,000 feet, the present height of the ramparts 20 feet. Depressions indicating earlier flint line shafts are clearly visible.*

the pattern of invasion, colonisation and settlement have probably been largely determined by such climatic changes.

Such a change of climate appears to have taken place during the next phase in the early history of Sussex—the Bronze Age. This was associated with a new group of immigrants from across the Channel, known as the Beaker Folk from the particular shape of their flat-bottomed drinking vessels, which are quite unlike the round-bottomed pottery of the Neolithic peoples. The latter was convenient for placing in the hot ashes of a hearth or in the hollow of an uneven floor, whereas the flat base would only rest securely on a flat surface. What may seem difficult to understand is why the round forms gave place so completely to the flat-bottomed form. The answer, which is equally applicable to small objects such as jewellery or large structures such as houses, is the general tendency to follow the fashions set by a ruling class or group whether established by conquest from without, or assimilated from within. The transition from the Neolithic to the Bronze Age could be either.

12 *Bronze-Age settlement, Itford*

The Bronze Age is also linked with a return to colder, drier conditions; the downland became less hospitable; while the forests of the Weald, which had flourished during the Neolithic period, provided a more attractive shelter. Whatever the reasons the Bronze-Age population spread itself more widely over the Weald, and there is rather less evidence of occupation of the now bleak and windswept Downs. Flint mining, however, continued since bronze implements were few and highly prized. The general way of life was not very different in the Bronze Age from the Neolithic. In both cases we must imagine small, isolated farms, such as two partly excavated on the side of Black Patch, near Findon. Both had extensive livestock enclosures for cattle, sheep, goats and pigs. Besides the single farms there were settlements such as those uncovered in 1955-56 on Itford Down, with as many as ten to twenty separate households, and others on the northern outskirts of Brighton at Downsview.

Other groups led a semi-nomadic existence, following their herds from place to place. The standard form of house was a round conical hut, about twenty feet across, with a central hearth and opening in the roof for the smoke to escape. Cremation took the place of burial and the remains were interred in round tumuli in contrast with the long mounds of the Neolithic period. Some were very large, such as the one destroyed at Palmeira Avenue, Hove, in the 19th century. The amber cup and polished double headed axe and whetstone from this burial are now amongst the most treasured objects in the Brighton Museum. The amber cup suggests trade contacts across the North Sea, and the axe and whetstone were probably symbols of high office, such as the mace and sceptre of a later age.

Other large examples survive on Bow Hill, and there are six in line— known as the Devil's Jumps—on Monkton Down near Treyford. Mostly, however, they were small, and altogether nearly a thousand have so far been identified in the area, chiefly on the higher slopes of the chalk, and on the lower Greensand hills that surround the Weald clay. Occasionally a Bronze-Age burial site has been discovered accidentally, as when a farmer

13 *Bronze-Age beaker*

14 *The excavation of a Bronze-Age barrow at West Heath near the Hampshire border.*

ploughing near the summit of the Round Hill, Steyning, sliced through the tops of some twenty burial urns. Although bronze tools were scarce and valuable, and flint continued to serve for most purposes, some large hoards of bronze—mostly socketed and flanged axes and spearheads—have been found, notably at Black Rock, near Brighton, at Bognor, and at Wilmington. These were probably buried by Bronze-Age smiths for safe keeping, and for some reason never recovered.

Since the first edition of this history, a remarkable Bronze-Age burial site has been excavated in the heart of the Weald, on a sandstone ridge, midway between Horsham and Crawley. It proved to be unique in the south east of England. Within a circular mound, measuring nearly a hundred feet across, two concentric circles of massive stones were uncovered. These were all that remained of circular dry-stone walling denuded by centuries of ploughing and twice broken into by grave robbers, or by amateur archaeologists—once in the Roman period, and again in the 18th century. A significant feature was that nearly two hundred Roman coins were found scattered at various levels in the earth cover. It is clear that this burial mound, built perhaps fifteen centuries earlier, commemorating some chieftain of the early Bronze Age, had continued as a place of veneration into Roman times—treated perhaps not unlike the wishing wells associated with Christian saints of a later period. Unfortunately, a condition of excavation was that the site should be cleared for agriculture, and not a trace now remains.

In this same region a number of other Bronze-Age sites such as at West Heath on the West Sussex/Hampshire border have been identified, and there are some grounds for assuming that the central Weald was more generally settled and utilised in this period than it has previously been supposed. There is, in fact, more evidence of Bronze- and Iron-Age settlement within the Weald than of later Saxon.

15 *Amber cup, Hove*

3

Iron-Age Hill Forts and the Roman Conquest

The general way of life of the Bronze Age, which lasted for well over a thousand years with little change, was disturbed by the coming of the Celts from the south-east. This was certainly no sudden event, such as the Roman conquest five hundred years later, or that of the Normans over fifteen hundred years later. It was a rather slow infiltration. The first settlers may have come peaceably as coastal colonists prepared to trade with the existing peoples on the Downs and in the Weald. They came from the south-east and the first settlements were in the eastern part of the county. It may be significant also that at about this time a damper and warmer climatic period returned.

Over a period of time other Celtic groups followed. Traffic with the Continent became much more general. Flint, the material from which tools had previously been made, and more recently bronze, was now largely replaced by iron, and farming became more concerned with the growing of crops, less with semi-nomadic herding. This led to a more closely knit population with an increasing number of village communities. It is from this period that there is the earliest evidence of corn-drying kilns. A large number of these have been found in connection with agricultural settlements on the Downs. In all cases the domes which covered the drying chambers have disintegrated, but the furnace chambers underneath the large stone slabs, which form the floors of the drying compartments, remain intact with soot encrustation and usually a great deal of half incinerated grain. The latter has provided evidence of the type of corn grown. Many pits for the storage of the dried grain have also been found and, on the basis of the evidence now collected, an attempt to reproduce an Iron-Age Farm was made at Butser Down just beyond the Sussex/Hampshire border and now at Chalton. This helps us to estimate the agricultural yield, and therefore the size of the population which might have been maintained within any given area known to have been cultivated in this period. The experiment includes not only cereal growing using the iron-age-type plough, but also livestock—early breeds of sheep, cattle and pigs—and the construction and decay of Iron-Age houses.

The Celts were warlike and, although there is no reason to believe that they drove out the existing inhabitants, they soon became the dominant element. With their coming, new areas were opened up for settlement, particularly in the Weald.

16   *Corn drying oven, Thunders barrow*

These developments culminated, in the third century B.C., in the building of relatively large hill-top sites enclosed by defence works that can still impress us by their scale and massive strength, as at Cissbury and the Trundle. The size of the fortifications—at Cissbury enclosing sixty acres, with an enclosing wall over a mile long—indicate that these places would have been both defence points for the whole of the surrounding area and visible symbols of power. These banks and ditches are impressive enough today, but the original fortifications with their revetments of massive timber must have been formidable. In one at least of these Iron-Age forts—that at Highdown—the revetments were reinforced with flint walls. This grouping of hill-top sites implies a social organisation on a tribal basis similar, no doubt, to that described by Julius Caesar as existing in Gaul two hundred years later. Sussex may therefore have been an area of occasional inter-tribal war during the time these forts were built.

Smaller Iron-Age fortified sites exist in other parts, not only in the downland, but also in the Weald. Several of these, such as the promontory fort at Henfield, have not yet been excavated, or their dates verified. The promontory fort near Iping was recognised from an air photograph taken when woodland was cleared in 1957. That the central Weald at this time was by no means uninhabited forest is clear from the great Iron-Age fort at Oldbury, constructed during the first century B.C., just across the Kentish boundary. This lies beside an important track which runs north from the coast near Hastings, past the new iron smelting area and on through the heart of the Weald into Kent.

17 *Iron Age*

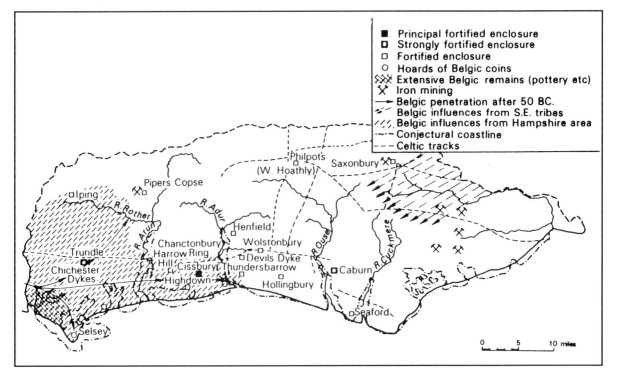

During the first century B.C. contacts with the Continent became still closer. In 75 B.C., people called the Belgae, of mixed Celtic and Germanic stock, invaded and occupied most of what is now Essex, Hertfordshire and part of Kent. This was followed twenty years later by the two expeditions of Julius Caesar, and the temporary occupation of the south-east by Roman legionaries. Though neither of these events touched Sussex directly, the indirect consequences were considerable. Iron-Age strongholds such as Mount Caburn were strengthened, and there would certainly have been an influx of refugees from the north and north-east. Four years after Caesar's second expedition, an invasion by the Belgic tribe of the Atrebates, landing first in the Isle of Wight and Hampshire, had within a few years overrun the Manhood peninsula of Sussex—the Manhood peninsula is the name given to the area extending south from the Trundle to Selsey. Leading this invasion was Commius, an Atrebatian who had been sent to Britain as an envoy before Caesar's first expedition in 55 B.C. Commius therefore knew Britain well, and no doubt had useful contacts in the area.

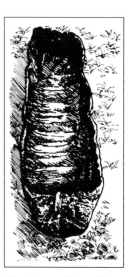

18 *Dug-out boat, River Arun*

Soon after the Belgic occupation of the Manhood peninsula, a Belgic centre of some importance may have been established a few miles to the south of where Chichester now stands. Judging by the amount of pottery, coins and jewellery, which at various times has been found on the beaches between Selsey and Wittering, it is likely that this town was later washed away by the sea. This would explain the lack of any trace of the actual site. Evidence of other sites at Lavant and Westhampnett, to the north and east of Chichester, has also been discovered. A 10-km line of earthworks running from east to west, north of Chichester—the 'Chichester Dykes'—was constructed. Although the line is not continuous, the gaps may originally have been filled by natural obstacles. Its function is not clear. It is too long to be manned and may best be seen as a territorial demarcation around an oppidum which may have been under Chichester or perhaps in the Fishbourne area. Excavations in 1958-59 strengthened the view that some at least were Belgic work, with the defences facing north. Excavations on the east terminal in 1983 also indicate a late Iron-Age date but an immediate post-conquest date cannot be ruled out.

Immediately prior to the Claudian invasion of Britain in A.D. 43 this area was ruled by Verica who appears to have been under pressure from the Catuvellauni under Cunobelin to the north. His fleeing to Rome to seek assistance is seen to be one of the reasons for Claudius' invasion.

Agriculture was widely practised, not only on the coastal plain, but also on the downland. A survey, for instance, of the remains of Celtic field boundaries on the Downs behind Brighton between the Adur and the Ouse has revealed more than thirty Iron-Age hamlets, most of which would certainly have been established by the time of the Roman Conquest. Very many of these ancient field boundaries, revealed so clearly in air photographs, have, over the last few years, been completely obliterated by deep ploughing—in most cases the first disturbance for fifteen hundred years.

Further to the east, beyond the Pevensey Levels, which then formed a wide inland estuary separating the hilly region between Bexhill and Rye

19 *The Romans con-*
nected Chichester to
London by building Stane
Street in about A.D. 70.
It is just over 57 miles in
length. Some of the best
preserved sections can be
found at Eartham and are
owned by the National
Trust.

from the rest of Sussex, the population was relatively sparse, except for the iron-working districts to the north of Hastings. There is no evidence of a port of any importance at that time in eastern Sussex although the Caburn itself must have sloped down directly to the wide, navigable estuary of the Ouse. In 1965 during work on the banks of the Arun to mitigate flooding the remains of six boats hollowed from the trunks of large oaks were found between Burpham and Pulborough. One must have been well over thirty feet long. Their dating has to be confirmed by carbon-14 tests, but it seems probable that some at least date from the pre-Roman period, although this technique of boat making may have continued into a later age.

Sussex, or at least that part which was later included in the kingdom of Cogidubnus, played a significant rôle in the actual conquest of Britain. The Romans had a number of friendly contacts amongst the British leaders. Whenever possible they pursued the policy of 'divide and rule'. After the invasion it seems likely that they installed Cogidubnus as a local client King to look after Rome's interests in the area previously ruled by Verica. There is nothing to suggest that he was unsuccessful in this. The area is referred to in Roman documents as 'The Kingdom' (Regnum). Tacitus, writing some fifty years later the biography of his uncle, Agricola, the first great governor of the new Roman province of Britain, says: Certain states were presented to King Cogidubnus, who maintained his unswerving loyalty down to our own times—an example of the long-established Roman custom of employing even kings to make others slaves'.

It was presumably Cogidubnus who founded Chichester, as the local capital, conveniently astride the coast road from Havant to Portslade, Stane Street being constructed to link it directly with Londinium, the new commercial centre of Britain. Significantly, the Roman name given to Chichester was Noviomagus or 'Newmarket'.

One of the most interesting discoveries from this early period of the Roman occupation is the so-called 'Cogidubnus Stone', now let into the wall under the arcade of the Assembly Rooms in North Street. This was dug up in 1723, not far from its present position. Part of the lettering was destroyed, but sufficient is left to reconstruct the inscription which, translated, reads: 'To Neptune and Minerva this Temple is dedicated for the welfare of the divine House by the authority of Tiberius Claudius Cogidubnus, Great King in Britain, by members of the Guild of Smiths' (or possibly shipwrights). Shipbuilding was probably an important industry in the area.

4

The Roman Occupation

We cannot be precise about the sequence of events in Sussex during the first years of the Roman occupation. The excavation during the 1960s of a great Roman palace at Fishbourne suggests that here was an important administrative and supply base which must have played a considerable part in the earlier phases of Roman conquest and consolidation. Certainly the foundation of Chichester and the construction of the roads radiating from there to Clausentum (Bitterne, Southampton) in the west, to Calleva Atrebatum (Silchester) to the north, and Londinium in the north-east, took place very soon after the conquest of the south and south-east. Sussex escaped the ravages of the rising led by Boudicca, and later, while the extreme north was being subdued and the northern defence system in the lowlands of Scotland perfected by Agricola, development was rapid in the south. The amphitheatre for example, at Chichester, was almost certainly built between A.D. 80 and 90. This amphitheatre was identified in 1935 when a depression in the ground was noticed some hundred yards to the south-east of the city wall. Excavations revealed a stone wall, in places ten to twelve feet high,

20 *The Roman walls surrounding Chichester date back to the third century, and run for one and a half miles, forming an irregular polygon around the City. They were originally built of earth with a facing of flint and mortar, with two ditches beyond them. The walls we see today are medieval, based on the Roman foundation. During the fourth century, the Romans strengthened the City's defences by building bastions.*

27

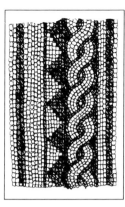

21 *Mosaic border, Bignor*

22 *Roman occupation*

plastered and painted possibly to resemble marble, and enclosing an area measuring 56.39 x 45.72 metres. It is now built over, and to quote S.E. Winbolt: 'The vandals could not find it in their hearts or purses to spare the only known Roman amphitheatre in the County of Sussex'.

Excavation of the town itself has been intermittent and often frustrating, since the present city lies exactly over the Roman site, and with Chester preserves better than any other existing English city the basic Roman plan. A few bombed sites have contributed some useful information since the war, but many of the important Roman buildings, such as the Forum and the Basilica, lying under later buildings such as the cathedral, are unlikely ever to be completely revealed.

Just outside the city the foundations have been uncovered of the largest domestic Roman building to be found in Britain. This is on the site of the early invasion base at Fishbourne. Some two-thirds of the site has been excavated, the rest being under a number of houses, gardens and a main road. It consisted of four wings surrounding a central formal garden constituting what can only be described as a palace or administrative centre rather than a great house. It was evidently planned soon after Fishbourne had served its purpose as a military supply base, and it is possible that it may have been built for or by Cogidubnus. The palace was completed well before the end of the first century and like the planning of Chichester was

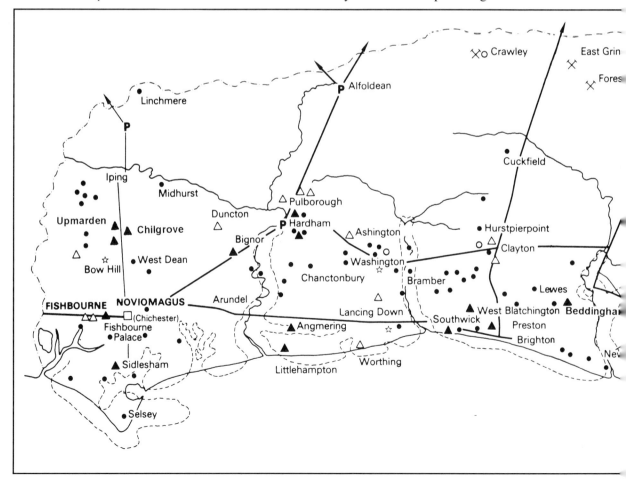

part, no doubt, of the Roman policy of impressing the native population by the magnificence of their urban culture and technology. What happened to this building in the second century is less clear. Various modifications were made, some implying a decline in importance, such as the splitting up of larger into smaller rooms. Readjustments of this kind were in fact being carried out when the fire occurred which destroyed the building and apparently led to its almost total abandonment in the late third century. The palace at Fishbourne has now become one of the best known archaeological sites in Britain and thousands of people visit the mosaic pavements and the formal garden which has been restored to something of its original appearance.

Evidence from the hundreds of Roman coins found in Chichester also points to the latter part of the first century A.D. and to most of the second century as the period of greatest activity and prosperity, which fits in with the general pattern of Imperial policy. This was to develop towns as quickly as possible as centres for the dissemination of Roman culture, and as embodiments of Roman ideals and authority. The existing walls are medieval, but rest on Roman foundations. The first Roman defences date from the end of the second century and comprise an earth rampart and ditch. At the end of the third century the city walls were rebuilt and strengthened with strong bastions at regular intervals.

23   Roman   bastion, Chichester

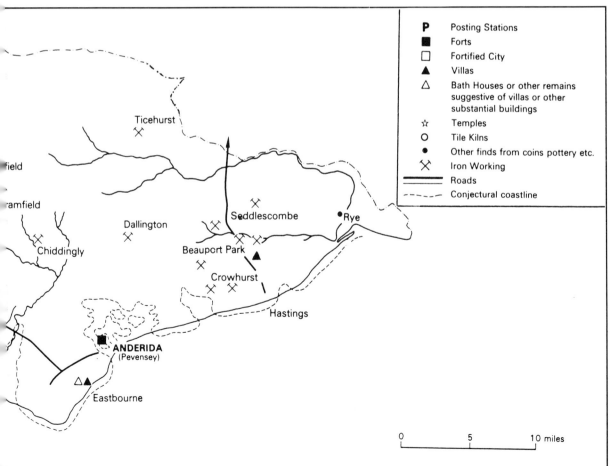

The strengthening of Chichester's defences was part of a carefully conceived system of garrison forts, built at this time round the south-east from Caister in Norfolk to Carisbrook in the Isle of Wight. These coastal defences were placed under a new officer entitled *Comes Litoris Saxonici* (Count of the Saxon shore). The main garrison post in Sussex was at Anderida (Pevensey). Whereas Chichester was a fortified town occupying 90 acres, Pevensey was a fort enclosing approximately nine acres and protecting a town the site of which has been lost, possibly in later inundations by the sea. But no one visiting the Roman fort today can fail to be impressed by it. There is certainly no sign yet of faltering workmanship or failure to match a sense of design with monumental strength. The walls form an oval, and to that extent the plan differs from those of all the other forts in this coastal series. This was no doubt dictated by the site, which was an irregular peninsula stretching into the estuary which came close to the walls on three sides. In later centuries the sea eroded and destroyed the southern side: still later it began to recede, assisted in the Middle Ages by the gradual enclosure of the mud flats by sea walls, and by drainage. Today Pevensey lies stranded some four miles from the coast.

The rapid development and prosperity of Sussex in the early days of the Roman occupation is supported by other evidence, such as that of villas at Angmering, Arundel, Pulborough and Southwick, which were built in the second half of the first century A.D. Presumably these were built for members of the local aristocracy.

The earlier iron industry was greatly expanded by the Romans. The evidence is in the enormous quantities of furnace slag used as hard core in the road that crosses near Maresfield, north across the Surrey border to Edenbridge: and in the mounds of Roman slag at Beauport Park near Battle. One of these covered two acres, was fifty feet high, and crowned with trees. In the 19th century these mounds were completely levelled when they were used as material for road making. Associated with this iron working was a large bath house which has survived in places. Many of the tiles from the site were stamped CLBR suggesting that it was controlled by the Classis Britannica, the Roman fleet in Britain.

The coastal plain, the Downs, and the Greensand hills were already settled before the Romans came; we can assume some improvements in agricultural techniques, and possibly the establishment of some efficiently managed agricultural estates during Roman times. Recent excavations of a villa at West Blatchington revealed a basilica-like building with house and storage rooms presumably under one roof, a reminder of the great composite house and farm buildings of Friesland today. Close to this building, 11 ovens for corn drying were also found, suggesting a large farm centre. Buildings of a very large size were added at the end of the third century to the precincts of the villa at Bignor—one almost 200 feet in length. Whether these were barns, or built to house livestock, large-scale agriculture is implied.

Most farming, however, on the Downs and elsewhere, was carried on as before by small farmers owning and cultivating their fields individually, and

24 *The Roman Villa at Bignor was discovered in 1811. Sited close to Stane Street, the villa was, by the fourth century, built to an exceptionally high standard and contains some of the country's best preserved mosaics* above left.

25 *The mid-second century 'Cupid on a dolphin' mosaic at the Fishbourne Roman Palace,* above right.

26 *Model of the conjectural reconstruction of the Palace looking west; the main entrance is in the middle foreground. The audience chamber, or hall of justice, faces the entrance on the far side.*

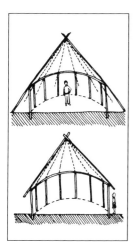

27 *Alternative interpretations of post hole evidence*

living in scattered hamlets. Occasionally they would visit Chichester, or the nearest market, to sell their produce, and to buy pottery, farm equipment, or perhaps some exotic import from the Mediterranean, and attend shows which might be staged in theatre or amphitheatre there. Visits might be made to one of the hill-top shrines, such as that on Lancing Down, Bow Hill, or Chanctonbury, but even these small Roman places of pilgrimage were almost certainly on the site of pre-existing Celtic temples. Religious observance, both before, during and after the Roman occupation, combined very satisfactorily a pleasurable outing with the sense of an observance performed.

Posting stations simplified journeys to London or further afield. These were provided with mansions, inns and stables where horses could be changed. Two on Stane Street are situated in Sussex, approximately eleven miles apart—the first at Hardham, just south of Pulborough, the second at Alfoldean, two miles south-west of Horsham. Quick transport, or the delivery of letters along such roads was very efficiently organised, and unequalled until the mail coach and turnpike system of the early 19th century. A posting station similar to those on Stane Street has been identified on the Chichester-Silchester road at Iping, but it has not yet been excavated. Inhabitants of Sussex felt themselves not only an integral part of the Roman empire, but very closely linked with the peoples across the Channel; in the country as well as in the towns Latin was understood, and the urban population was certainly bilingual. Both the Celtic speech of Sussex and Latin were spoken by fellow Celts in Gaul. There was, in fact, far less sense of division than there is today.

Houses and Farmsteads from earliest times to the Saxon Conquest

Our knowledge of the kind of dwellings in which most of the population lived up to the early Middle Ages is based almost entirely on archaeological evidence, found, usually, by accident. The second difficulty is that survival in the ground depends largely on the nature of the subsoil. In acid bog conditions, as in the marshes round Glastonbury, wood, leather and even cloth can survive for thousands of years, whereas from the lime areas such as the chalk, post holes and pits may be perfectly preserved, but every bit of wood, leather or cloth will have disintegrated long ago. In the clay and sandy loams which cover the main part of the Sussex Weald and the Coastal Plain, and where the ground has been deeply ploughed throughout subsequent centuries, neither post holes nor material are likely to remain. Here, apart from burial mounds, only the solid deep set foundations of important Roman buildings have any chance of survival.

Another difficulty is that there is often more than one possible interpretation of the general plan or even shape of a building. A circular arrangement of post holes may be of posts forming the outer walls of a hut, but they may equally be supporting long rafters which continued to the ground, but left no trace. The second interpretation would more than double the area covered by the hut. There are also many questions of detail. Misinterpretations can lead to an underestimation not only of the craftsmanship but also of possibly

I   *The Sussex Downs stretch from the Hampshire border near South Harting in the west, to Beachy Head near Eastbourne in the east and are designated as an Area of Outstanding Natural Beauty. The coastline of the Downs, such as here at the Seven Sisters between the mouth of the River Cuckmere and the Birling Gap, has been designated as Sussex Heritage Coast.*

II   *The River Cuckmere meanders before it reaches the sea at Cuckmere Haven. The area forms part of the Seven Sisters Country Park.*

III *Amberley Castle—a residence of the Bishops of Chichester, built during the late 14th century, when southern England was under threat from French raids. The north facing curtain wall overlooks marshland and water meadows known as the Amberley Wild Brooks.*

IV *Herstmonceux Castle. Built between 1440 and 1447, the castle was the first building of any size to be built of brick in England since Roman times. The interior was dismantled in 1777, but was restored between the Wars. After the Second World War until recently it was the home of the Royal Observatory.*

V *Bodiam Castle was built in 1385 when the country was under threat from French raids. It was built to a model design for the time and had a harbour navigable from the River Rother. The interior, now a hollow shell, was 'slighted' by Waller in 1643.*

decorative elements in early buildings. This is the kind of problem which should make us accept only tentatively suggested reconstructions whether we are dealing with the remote past or any period before the Middle Ages. With these provisos in mind it can be said that the considerable amount of research done in Sussex during the last decades does enable us to build up some idea of changing house styles in these early centuries.

The nomadic hunters, who for three or four thousand years wandered over the Weald in the mesolithic period, left innumerable flint implements to mark their temporary settlements and journeys, but little to help us to reconstruct their dwellings. Hollow pits associated with their implements have been interpreted as their dwelling sites, and one such has been preserved just over the northern border of the county at Abinger in Surrey. A reconstruction of a bivouac supported on forked poles based on two post holes seems to be the most probable form of roof. Where archaeological evidence is lacking, however, we can sometimes be justified in assuming that very early ways of building may in fact survive under similar conditions of life into a later age. Charcoal burners, for example, in the Weald, right up to the Second World War, lived in simple conical huts of turf supported on a wooden frame. Such huts leave absolutely no trace in the ground after even a few decades. It is not unreasonable to suppose that our early ancestors, men of the Middle Stone Age, built huts as well constructed, or even that the method of building may have passed down without much alteration from those days until the present day.

With the colonisation of Sussex by Neolithic farmers we are perhaps on slightly more certain ground, though in Sussex no remains of houses have yet been found with the possible exception of post holes at Whitehawk which could be interpreted as a hut. But elsewhere in Britain, and on the Continent, a number of Neolithic sites have been explored in which the foundations, both of stone and timber buildings, have been identified. Almost all are rectangular and some of the Continental ones are of considerable length; many have supporting aisle posts, and seem to have been divided into a large number of smaller compartments. For this reason it has been assumed that they housed an extended family—three or four generations with married brothers and sisters sharing the one building, and that some part of these buildings may have been used as byres, and to house livestock.

For the Bronze Age there is now a good deal of evidence, and a number of discoveries have added much to our knowledge. They confirm a pattern of scattered farmsteads consisting of small groupings of approximately round huts surrounded by a stockade, but a number of questions remain unanswered. The most completely explored site in Sussex—on the Downs above Itford near Lewes—consisted of 13 huts, some of which were almost certainly for storage, but how far the larger huts were occupied by one family is not clear, so that the actual size of the community is conjectural. The second uncertainty is how long such a settlement lasted, since replacement of timbers could be made without noticeable disturbance or the digging of fresh post holes. An excavation of the site of two late Bronze-Age houses on Amberley Mount in 1958 proved the existence of another

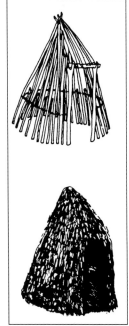

28 *Framework of charcoal burner's turf hut*

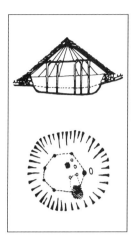

29 *Bronze-Age hut, Amberley Mount*

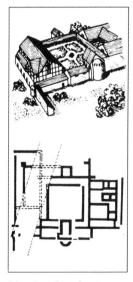

30 *Southwick, Roman villa*

type of house, built on a terrace of sloping chalk and sunk slightly in the ground, anticipating the more deeply sunken huts built by the Saxons more than a thousand years later. It is assumed that the posts must have been supports for the rafters, the ends of which would have rested on the ground; otherwise in these sunken houses, if the posts had formed the outside walls, the hollowed space outside would in wet weather have become a quagmire and the house itself a pond. It is also necessary to remember that all our evidence of house design in this period has so far come from the chalk area of the Downs, and it may be quite wrong to assume a similar pattern of buildings in the Weald.

In the Iron Age both round and rectangular houses are found. The former is typical of the first millennium B.C. Some have no post holes and must have been stake built. A settlement of round houses and four-, six- and eight-post structures, possibly granaries, has recently been excavated on the Downs near Lavant. Work on Mount Caburn in 1932 established the fact that seventy or so hollows, clearly identified within the ramparts, were probably all storage pits for corn, those excavated measuring from three to eight feet in depth and diameter. These, it was assumed, were attached to individual houses. Fragments of daub with wattle imprint were found, and some door latches; but the actual size and shape of such dwellings can only be determined by systematic excavation.

With the Romans came new techniques of building, and entirely new house plans, both in town and country villas. The simplest form was a rectangular block containing three or more rooms. A development of this involved the erection of short wings at each end with a linking corridor. Further developments led to the addition of wings completely enclosing a central courtyard, as in the final phase of the impressive villa at Bignor. However in Sussex there is clear evidence for some very early villas that are based on Italian-style villas. Fishbourne and Southwick are two examples. The villa at Southwick was of the completely enclosed courtyard type. In the early 1990s excavations at Beddingham Roman Villa near Lewes resulted in a number of important discoveries, including a Bronze-Age cemetery, an Iron-Age round house and occupation in the Roman period. Between the 1960s and 1980s in the valley leading north-west from Chichester, close to the line of the Roman road from Chichester to Silchester, two Roman villas were discovered near Chilgrove. Probably the majority of the Roman villas were centres of large agricultural estates; almost all have hypocaust systems of underfloor heating, and at least one or two rooms with mosaic paving. Quite clearly they were the houses, whether of natives or immigrants, of a sophisticated and cultured class.

In a town such as Chichester most of the dwellings would have been compressed versions of the courtyard villas of the countryside with a much smaller piazza or enclosed area, in some cases with a shared dividing wall between neighbours. Frequently there would be two storeys, while its country equivalent would have only one. The bulk of the population in the countryside would continue to build and to live as they had done before the Roman conquest.

5

Saxon Sussex

Between the years A.D. 400 and 410 the Roman legions, coastal garrisons and naval forces were withdrawn to defend the Continent against the Teutonic armies which had broken through the northern defences of the Empire. The first record of Saxon landings in Sussex occurs in the Anglo-Saxon Chronicle under the year A.D. 477. The dates given in the Chronicle are now considered to be 20 years too early, so 477 becomes 457. It reads: 'This year came Aella to Britain, with his three sons, Cymen, Wlenking and Cissa, in three ships: landing at a place that is called Cymenshore. There they slew many of the Welsh; and some in flight they drove into the wood that is called Andred'sley.' (The 'Welsh' here, of course, refers to the Romano-British inhabitants.) What happened in the seventy years between these dates?

31 *Glass goblet, High-down, Saxon burial*

It is probable that Sussex, as part of the Saxon Shore, was garrisoned by Germanic mercenaries. However by the time Aella arrived in the middle of the century it is likely that this defence strategy would not have been as effective.

From the close of the fourth century, it seems likely that successive raids and insecurity led to the abandonment of the larger villas, and the migration of many of the town dwellers from such places as Chichester to the west, or even across the channel to Brittany. The way would thus be paved for the final invasion and occupation by the Saxons. The actual conquest and settlement took place over a lengthy period. The distribution of known Saxon burial sites suggests that there may have been a good deal of fighting in the area between Shoreham and Pevensey. Grave objects such as a highly wrought brooch display a high level of craftsmanship, however barbaric in design by Roman standards. A perfectly preserved incised glass vase with an inscription in Greek was found in the early Saxon cemetery on Highdown Hill to the north-east of Worthing. It could have only been made in the eastern Mediterranean, and suggests loot from a Roman site—clearly such objects were highly valued.

The next entry relating to Aella in the Anglo-Saxon Chronicle is under the year 485 and reads: 'This year Aella fought with the Welsh nigh Mecred's-Burnstead.' Where was this place? No one has yet satisfactorily identified it. The next entry is five years later, under the year 490: 'This year Ella and Cissa besieged the city of Andred, and slew all that were therein, nor was one Briton left there afterwards'. Just as the Iron-Age fortress of Cissbury had been rebuilt five centuries before, to meet the Belgic advance and later

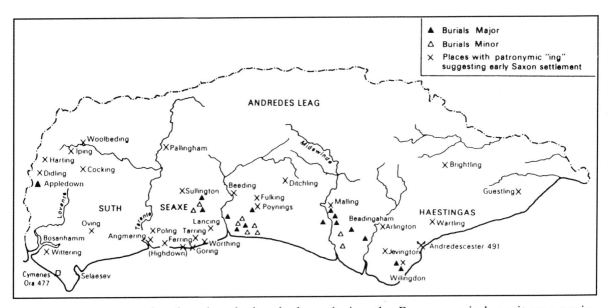

ANDREDES LEAG

▲ Burials Major
△ Burials Minor
✕ Places with patronymic "ing"
   suggesting early Saxon settlement

✕ Woolbeding
✕ Iping
✕ Harting
✕ Didling   ✕ Cocking
▲ Appledown

✕ Pallingham

Midwinde

SUTH   SEAXE
Oving   ✕ Sullington   Beeding
✕   ✕ Fulking
Bosanhamm Lancing   ✕ Poynings
✕ Wittering Angmering ✕ Poling Tarring ✕   Malling
           ✕ Ferring ✕ ✕ Worthing Beadingaham
Cymenes   Selaesev   (Highdown) Goring   ✕ Arlington
Ora 477

✕ Ditchling

✕ Brightling
Guestling ✕

HAESTINGAS
✕ Wartling

✕ Jevington
Andredescester 491
Willingdon

32 *Saxon Sussex,*
Pagan period c.477-682

abandoned and ploughed up during the Roman period, so it was again, hastily but less efficiently, refortified to meet the new threat. Other forts also received this treatment.

Beyond Pevensey, estuary and marsh divided the Hastings area from the west. What took place there is completely undocumented, but the area appears to have been invaded and occupied by a separate group of Saxons—the Haestingas. These gave their name to Hastings, and continued a semi-isolated and independent existence for nearly two hundred years until the year 771, when it is recorded that Offa of Mercia subdued the kingdoms of Kent and Sussex, and 'the men of Hastings'.

Aella himself was recognised as a leader of more than local importance, since he is recorded in the Anglo-Saxon Chronicle as the first 'Bretwalda' (Broad-Wielder) or vaguely accepted overlord of all the Saxon invaders. Yet Sussex appears to have remained until the seventh century singularly isolated from the rest of England. The wealden forest became a more effective barrier than it had been to Celt or Roman. Stane Street and the other wealden highways were abandoned, and there is no evidence even of Saxon iron workings. How then, in view of the rather scanty evidence, should we visualise the changes in Sussex during these two centuries?

First we must conclude that the existing Romano-Celtic population was almost completely driven out of the colonised area. With very few exceptions place names and names of physical features are Saxon: only a few Roman names and words persisted, such as Chichester (Cissa's 'Castra' or fort), or Andredswald (i.e. the forest of Anderida). Secondly the whole pattern and character of settlement was altered. The Saxons were forest plain and valley dwellers, they used a heavy two-yoke plough and worked their fields on a communal basis, sharing the great open fields which surrounded their closely built and centrally-placed village. Thus the Celtic upland farms and hamlets on the Downs decayed, and settlement was concentrated more completely on the coastal plain, the valleys, and along the Greensand belt under the north side of the Downs. There is little evidence that the Saxons occupied existing towns or villages. They preferred small, compact communities to the more scattered Celtic type of farm and field.

When, therefore, St Wilfred landed near Selsey in the year 681 and by his preaching converted the South Saxons to Christianity, the Sussex landscape was very different from that which a visiting Roman would have observed two or three centuries earlier. Bede, in his *Ecclesiastical History of England*, completed within a few years of Wilfred's death, gives a vivid account of the conversion of the South Saxons, embroidered with some charming and appropriate miracles. The fact that it was over eight years previously that the neighbouring kingdom of Kent had been converted, and that Sussex alone of the Heptarchic (seven) kingdoms remained pagan, shows the extent of its isolation.

Bede speaks of: 'A certain monk of the Scottish nation, whose name was Dicul, who had a very small monastery, at the place called Bosanham, encompassed with the sea and woods, and in it five or six brothers, who served our Lord in poverty and humility; but none of the natives cared either to follow their course of life, or to hear their preaching.' Within the later Saxon church at Bosham is an underground chapel or semi-crypt, which, according to tradition, is on the site of this small monastery. It is probably near here that Wilfred first preached and carried out his mass baptisms. Soon afterwards Bede continues: 'King Ethelwalch of the South Saxons, gave to the most reverend Prelate Wilfred, land of eighty-seven families to maintain his company who were in banishment, which place is called Selsey, that is, the island of the seals ... Bishop Wilfred, having this place given him, founded therein a monastery.' This later became the centre of the south Saxon diocese, but nothing remains either of the original monastery, or of the Minster which was built later. The site is now certainly under the sea, for the peninsula of Selsey must in Wilfred's day have been several times its present size. Embedded in a modern memorial at the edge of the parish church at Selsey are two fragments of interlaced decorative stone carving. These may well have formed part of an early Saxon cross— the kind of cross of which many examples survive in the north of England, and which date from the early phase of conversion to Christianity, being set up in the open as centres for preaching the gospel and baptism before the building of more substantial churches.

Selsey, therefore, from the end of the seventh century, became one of the most important places in Sussex, and culturally the most important. During the eighth and ninth centuries other towns began to assume some prominence as market centres. The grass-grown streets of Roman Chichester re-emerged flanked by wooden Saxon houses. It is possible that by the end of the sixth century a royal estate existed at Kingsham just south of the town while places such as Pevensey, Steyning, Lewes and Hastings developed into towns of craftsmen and traders instead of villages of farmers. In all these towns, mints are recorded by the 10th century—a sure sign of an urban economy.

33 *Saxon brooch from Alfriston*

In the ninth century, however, there was a setback. Just as, four hundred years before, life in Roman Sussex had ebbed and stagnated through the continual threat from Saxon raiders, so, in the ninth century, the now settled and Christianised Saxons suffered the same insecurity at the hands of the Danes. It is particularly difficult for a scattered farming community to meet the sudden attacks of mobile forces whose families and lands lie across the water, and who are perfectly equipped for rapid movement. For nearly fifty years, from 852 when parts of Kent were plundered, fear and uncertainty set back any further social and economic progress, though it did lead indirectly to the consolidation of the West Saxon monarchy and the integration of Sussex into this larger unit, which we can begin to think of as England, although it still excluded much of the West Country and the North.

Alfred the Great, King of the West Saxons, who finally checked the Danish conquest, endeavoured to meet these difficulties of defence and it was almost certainly he who inaugurated the building of a series of forts to be garrisoned at the threat of danger by men drawn from the surrounding population. The Burghal Hidage, a document of the early 10th century, lists these fortifications, called burhs, and the areas responsible for their main-tenance. There were five in Sussex; Hastings, Lewes, Burpham, Chichester and a place called 'Heorepeburan'—possibly Pevensey. Chichester had the largest supporting area, and the Roman walls were its defence. The Anglo-Saxon Chronicle under the year 895 records that: The Danish Army went up plundering in Sussex nigh Chichester; but the townsmen put them to flight, and slew many hundreds of them, and took some of their ships.' This

34 *Saxon Sussex after* must refer to the men who gathered at Chichester from the surrounding
conversion to Christianity area—it can hardly mean that the actual townsmen were sufficiently
682-1066 numerous to gain a victory on this scale.

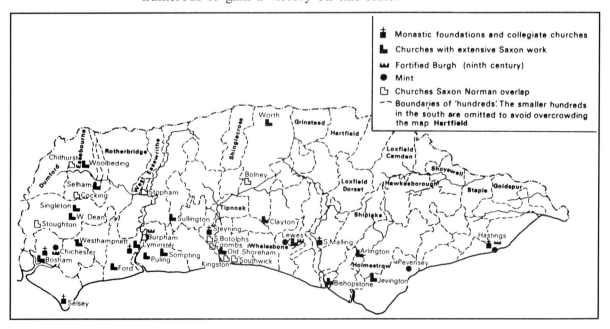

A measure of security was restored, for a few decades, in the mid-10th century. During the reign of King Edgar and the wise administration of the Church by St Dunstan, Archbishop of Canterbury, some of the ravages caused by the Danish raids were repaired. Several of the stone Saxon churches of Sussex may date from this period—built perhaps on the ashes of wooden churches destroyed by Danish raiders. It was during this period that the territorial division known as the hundred emerges as the most important unit in local administration. Its origins are obscure, nor is it clear whether the term derives ultimately from a measurement of land or of population. In Sussex there were 61, varying considerably in size; their boundaries even by the time of the Norman Conquest appear only approximately settled. What we do know is that the hundred, from the 10th century onwards, became important not only as a court of justice equivalent at least to the County Court and the Quarter Sessions, but also dealt with many matters which would now be the concern of one of the departments of the county council, such as highways or police. The meeting-place of the courts was at some central point within the hundred, often recorded in the name of the hundred, such as the bridge over the Rother—Rotherbridge hundred, or Tippa's Oak—Tipnoak hundred, or the hundred of Manhood.

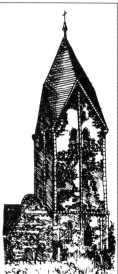

35 *Saxon tower, Sompting*

Another division which dates from Saxon times is, of course, the parish. This was an ecclesiastical division and new parishes were created and older ones subdivided throughout the Saxon period, as new churches were built. But in the more settled areas, most of the parish boundaries would have been defined well before the end of the Saxon period. The pattern that survives today, in spite of some rearrangement in the last hundred years or so, provides a clue to the character and size of the original Saxon communities. The long narrow parishes, for example, which stretch north and south under the ridge of the Downs, indicate the care with which land of different quality—chalk, greensand, gault and weald clay—were included in each settlement, the villages themselves being mostly sited on the dry shelf of the upper greensand, where the springs gush from the base of the chalk escarpment. Centuries later in the Tudor period, the parish rather than the shire, the hundred or the manor, was to become the fundamental unit in the pattern of local government and administration, and remained so until the 19th century.

With the reign of Ethelred, the Danish terror returned, and some of the entries in the Anglo-Saxon Chronicle are terse and vivid: 'Thence they advanced, and brought the greatest evil that ever any army could do, in burning and plundering and manslaughter, not only on the sea-coast in Essex, but in Kent and in Sussex and in Hampshire' (A.D. 994); and again: 'and everywhere in Sussex, and in Hampshire, and also in Berkshire, they plundered and burned as their custom is' (A.D.1000). At last in 1016, after the death of Ethelred, the Saxon Witan chose the Dane Canute as their king. Peace thus secured, there followed a genuine, though limited, Saxon renaissance. It is to this brief period before the Norman Conquest that most of the stone-built Saxon churches in Sussex belong. Remains of nearly thirty of these survive, incorporated in later Norman or Gothic buildings.

36 *Capital, Selham*

37 *The Saxon church overlooking the harbour at Bosham, now primarily a recreational sailing centre in Chichester Harbour.*

We must, however, remember that timber had been for centuries the traditional building material of the Saxons, and there was plenty to hand in Sussex: so it is probable that the rebuilding of so many churches in stone was dictated as much by the vulnerability of wood, as by a belief that stone was necessarily a superior material. Unfortunately, no timber buildings from the Saxon period have survived, and we can only assess their probable quality from other evidence such as jewellery. Much of the Saxon masons' work in Sussex churches does suggest the rather unsure efforts of craftsmen, attempting to translate into stone motifs which they were used to carving with mastery in wood. Such examples can be seen in the chancel arch capitals at Selham, or in the tower arch capitals at Sompting. At the same time, in the great roll mouldings of the chancel and tower arches of churches such as Bosham, Sompting and Clayton, we can trace the influence of early Norman buildings such as Bernay. The Channel was already becoming a link instead of a barrier.

Farms and Village Settlements

The Saxons created the pattern of village settlement which lasted with little change for nearly a thousand years, and still forms the basic settlement structure through most of the county, except the central Weald. It is, nevertheless, surprising how little certainty there is when any attempt is made to reconstruct the details of their environment. Archaeological research has, however, brought to light some evidence in the Downland area for a particular type of Saxon building often described as a 'grubenhaus'—from the German, 'gruben' to dig. These buildings were sunk one to two feet into ground, depending on the nature of the subsoil, and they were approximately rectangular with a gabled roof of the simplest kind supported by rafters resting on a central ridge piece, itself supported on upright posts aligned down the middle of the building. Foundations for this type of building have been found over a very wide area of north-west Europe, as well as in many parts of England. It was a simple, yet practical method of construction wherever drainage was good, providing maximum internal height with a minimum of walling or timber for roofing. One of these was excavated at Bishopstone near Seaford in 1968 and dates from the fifth century. The other, a working hut for weavers, was excavated at Erringham, near Shoreham, in 1964, and dates from the ninth century. On the floor were two groups of 35 loom weights indicating that two large upright looms must have occupied most of the space. The fact that four centuries separated these two huts suggests that it was a form of construction which lasted throughout most of the Saxon period.

An extremely important addition to our knowledge of early Saxon settlements in this region was made at Chalton, by the excavation of a downland site just beyond the western boundary of the county. Contrary to the assumption that Saxon settlements were almost entirely in valley and lowland with easy access to water, the Chalton site was located along the plateau of a downland ridge. The move to the valley, where the church was later built, must have taken place long after conversion to Christianity. Further interesting discoveries of two Saxon cemeteries were made not far from Chalton during the 1980s on Appledown near Compton, dating from between the late fifth century and the seventh century to the early eighth century. Some of the graves were thought to be early Christian burials and may be part of the cemetery belonging to the remote downland church of Upmarden, located half a mile to the south.

At the Chalton site, although there is a sprinkling of 'gruben' or sunken huts, the main domestic buildings conform to a pattern recognisably similar to early medieval farm houses—namely, a central open hall with hearth, and rooms at either end. The dimensions of two of these houses so far uncovered compare very closely with those of larger farmhouses which still survive from the later Middle Ages, or which have been rediscovered in the early medieval deserted village of Hangleton, namely between forty and fifty feet in total length, and between eighteen and twenty in width. Unlike, however, the Hangleton buildings, all of which were built of flint rubble, these all seem to have been built of timber post construction. There is some evidence to suggest that the walls between the posts may have been of horizontal planks or halved logs secured in grooves in the sides of the upright posts. There is another possibility that they were halved logs placed vertically as in the well known church at Greenstead in Essex. There is no evidence of wattle and daub infill. The height of the walls, as well as the roof structure, must be conjectural. Whether at either end of the central hall there might have been an upper storey or loft, as in equivalent farmhouses of the later Middle Ages, is also unknown.

38 *Box frame—early drawing*

39 *Burning house, Hastings, Bayeux Tapestry*

A further feature of the village was the close proximity of buildings combined with a somewhat random arrangement and along what appears to be the main street. This also matches the site at Hangleton, and suggests a greater continuity and a more coherent tradition, dating from Saxon times, than has been previously assumed. This would also have been the pattern at Steyning, which was an important Saxon port on the River Adur. Ethelwulf, father of King Alfred, and St Cuthman are said to have been buried here.

Almost certainly the majority of Saxon buildings in village and farm continued the use of posts let into the ground as the normal form of construction, but in churches and better quality houses a more sophisticated and durable method, now usually described as the 'boxframe', was almost certainly used. For lack of evidence it has been quite unreasonably assumed that this type of construction was only introduced into the south-east after the Norman Conquest and was not used by the Saxons although previously practised by the Romano-British. In this method the whole frame work of the building consists of squared and interlocking timbers supported on a horizontal ground plate of timber on which everything else, roof, floor and wall panels, is attached or hung. Unless this type of construction was known and widely used in the more important buildings it is difficult to interpret the pilaster decorations on the walls of Woolbeding, or the tower of Sompting church. Such decoration seems to be so obviously a copying in stone of timber framing.

It is frequently stated that the Saxons favoured the form of building described as a 'long house', with an ancestry going back to Neolithic times— houses in which the domestic living quarters are situated at one end of the building, the byre and storage in the other, with only the simplest of divisions between the two parts, possibly just a slight change in floor levels, and man and beast using the same entrance door. Such houses would vary in size with the number of livestock, and they could be extended at either end. They are still to be found in parts of Denmark and Holland and north Germany—the area from which the Saxons came—but there is little evidence that combined house and byre was ever usual in Sussex, whatever may have been the case in counties further to the west. Here in Sussex, from such evidence as we have, the arrangement of farms seems always to have been that of dwellings separated from other farm buildings, whether byres, barns or stables. Of the 13 buildings uncovered in the abandoned medieval village of Hangleton, only one could be interpreted as possibly a longhouse. More examples need to be discovered before we are justified in considering the longhouse as anything but exceptional. We should remember, however, that from Aella's landing in Sussex to the Norman Conquest was very nearly six centuries—longer than from Chaucer's pilgrims to the present day, time enough for many changes in custom or for adaptations to a milder climate. The very fact that no one can be certain what the Sussex village or farm was like in Saxon times, or what changes may have taken place during these centuries, is some measure of the need for much more intensive archaeological research.

6

Norman Sussex

It was during the Norman period that Sussex attained its greatest importance in relation to other English counties. Not only was it intimately associated with the events leading to the Conquest, and with the Conquest itself, but for 150 years it was the main highway from England to the Continent—a bridge connecting the estates of the Norman nobility in England and Normandy. Its growth in population, in the importance of its ports, in the clearing and colonisation of the Weald after centuries of relative neglect, represented changes as great in their way as those that followed the Neolithic, Celtic, Roman or Saxon invasions.

Before describing these changes something should be said about the events leading to the Conquest in so far as they affected Sussex. From the early years of the 11th century contacts between England and Normandy had been developing. In 1001, Ethelred 'the Unrede' married Emma, the daughter of Richard the Fearless, Duke of Normandy. In 1013 he took sanctuary in the Norman abbey of Fécamp when in flight from Danish raiders, and in 1016 he gave the rich manor of Rameslie, which included much of Hastings, to this abbey. There was, therefore, long before the Norman invasion, a close connection between Hastings and Normandy and this may in part have determined the invasion plan of William the Conqueror.

At the other end of the county lies Bosham which a popular, though recent, tradition associates with the story of Canute's chair. Conceivably such a legend might have stemmed from the construction of groins for the protection of an anchorage or of a building such as a palace. The story first appears a hundred years after Canute's death.

Traditions very often have some real foundation, but there is also a temptation for antiquarians with strong local attachments and vivid imaginations to manufacture evidence to support their theories. Sussex has had its quota. The River Adur, for example, was given this name in the 16th century in order to support the identification of the Roman town of Portus Adurni with Shoreham, an identification for which there is not the slightest justification. As recently as 1911 occurred perhaps the most spectacular example of all time—the attempt to supply one of the missing links in the early evolution of man by the deliberate planting in a gravel pit at Piltdown (near Chailey) of fragments of a recent human skull near the doctored jawbone of a modern ape. Perhaps the most widely diffused of all local legends are the relatively harmless stories of underground passages stretching often for miles through (or under!) impossible obstacles and usually, though vaguely, associated with smugglers or monks (or both).

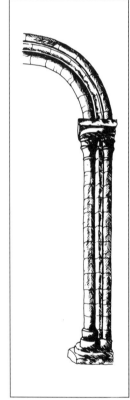

40 *Chancel arch, Bosham*

Although it is necessary to dissociate Canute from Bosham, the latter was certainly a favourite residence in Sussex of Godwin, Earl of Wessex and it was from here that Harold (Godwinson) sailed in 1064, an ill-fated voyage which ended in shipwreck and in his taking service with William Duke of Normandy in the war in Brittany. According to the Normans he then swore an oath of fealty to William, which he broke when, on his return to England, he accepted the crown on the death of Edward the Confessor.

All this is recorded pictorially in the Bayeux Tapestry. This vivid and dramatic account takes the form of an unbroken series of pictures passing without interruption from one event to the next and measures 210 feet in length by approximately two feet in height. The scenes include Harold praying in Bosham Church before sailing, the elaborate preparation of William's invasion fleet, its voyage and landing at Pevensey, the erection of a prefabricated wooden fort at Hastings, the burning of houses in Hastings, and other incidents, and conclude with the battle and the death of Harold.

41 The Bayeux Tapestry. William lands at Pevensey. Ships indicate little change in design from those used by the earlier Saxon and Danish invaders. Note the cavalry horses included in one of the ships.

This battle which altered the course of English history was fought on the hills behind Hastings in 1066. The Saxon army, wearied by a long march from Yorkshire, where Harold had utterly defeated a Danish invasion from the North Sea, had taken up trenched positions on ground through which the High Street of the town of Battle now runs. In the centre, and protecting the flanks, were some two or three thousand strongly-armed house-carls, but the bulk of the force consisted of poorly-armed levies from the south-eastern counties. Marshy ground separated the Saxon lines from the

Normans, who occupied the ridge to the south of where the Abbey now stands. This restricted the use of the cavalry which William had brought across with his invasion fleet. For hours the Normans failed to break the Saxon line, and it was not until the evening of this October day that victory was secured by two stratagems—a pretended flight which encouraged the heavy Saxon troops to break ranks and follow, and the shooting of arrows upwards, which, dropping from above, rendered useless the long Saxon body-shields. The victory was absolute. The conflict of perhaps 30,000 men, during eight hours, and at a total cost of a few thousand casualties, set England on a new course, and changed in particular the character and status of Sussex.

Although there seems to have been little further opposition in the south-east, in the north, in the south-west and in the Fens, sporadic resistance continued for several years. In Sussex, in view of its vital situation across the communication routes with Normandy, immediate measures had to be taken to secure these. For this reason Sussex was subdivided into rapes, or administrative divisions which ran north to south, each based on a port, and controlling one of the highways to the north. These rapes were given by William to five of his most trusted Norman barons. Strong castles were built to defend the harbours and ports and, along the routes which ran north, temporary garrison points of the wooden motte and bailey form were erected. The fact that most of these were abandoned some time before the close of the century indicates that any real danger from local risings or attacks, even in the forested areas of the Weald, were no longer feared.

42 A wooden castle is being built at Hastings on a mound which has been rapidly thrown up. At various strategic points in Sussex mottes of this type, housing small garrisons, were built immediately after the Conquest.

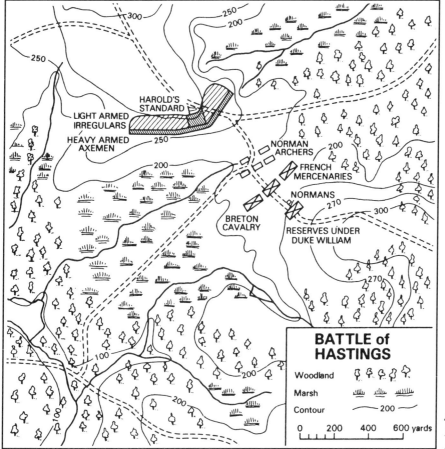

43 *Map of the Battle of Hastings.*

BATTLE of HASTINGS

Woodland		
Marsh		
Contour	—— 200 ——	

0   200   400   600 yards

Labels on map: HAROLD'S STANDARD, LIGHT ARMED IRREGULARS, HEAVY ARMED AXEMEN, NORMAN ARCHERS, FRENCH MERCENARIES, NORMANS, BRETON CAVALRY, RESERVES UNDER DUKE WILLIAM

44 *The site of the Battle of Hastings, below Battle Abbey.*

The most powerful of these feudal barons was Roger of Montgomery, who held the combined rapes of Chichester and Arundel. Chichester was both port and fortified garrison point, and the Norman castle mound can still be seen within the city walls in Priory Park. The route inland from Chichester was protected by the castle on St Anne's Hill, Midhurst, and temporary mottes probably at Selham and Verdley. At Arundel the Normans created what was virtually a new town, protected by a castle on the hills above. The present castle occupies the site of the original motte and bailey.

Within these rapes Roger held in all 83 manors, leased singly or in groups to lesser figures in the Norman hierarchy. Very few Saxon names are to be found in Sussex among those holding land in the Domesday Survey compiled 20 years later. Sussex would have been strongly represented at the Battle of Hastings since most of the last-minute reinforcements to the Saxon army must have been drawn from the immediate neighbourhood. The estates of all who fought at Hastings whether they survived or not were forfeited.

To the east of Arundel came the rape of William de Braose. His rape centred on the fortress of Bramber, which commanded the then wide estuary of the Adur, and protected the port of Steyning. Here again, before the end of the 11th century an entirely new town was created—at New Shoreham. One of the earliest buildings still standing in Sussex is the Marlipins in the centre of the town. Its original purpose is conjectural, but it most probably served as a kind of early customs house in which the port dues, paid in kind to the Lord of the Manor, were stored. In the 13th

45 Pevensey. Roman fortress and medieval castle from the west. The ruined Norman keep (astride the Roman wall) is enclosed by the medieval castle and moat. The Saxon village lies just beyond.

46 *Bramber Castle. A conjectural view drawn by Alan Sorrell of the Norman motte and bailey castle in the early 12th century. At this time the River Adur was navigable as far as Steyning, just beyond Bramber.*

century, before the prosperity of the port began to decline, it was given a new and striking checkerboard gothic-style façade of squared stone and knapped flint. The anchorage lay where meadows now separate the Saxon town of Old Shoreham from the new Norman town. Inland was built a line of garrison posts stretching from Edburton Hill to Knepp near West Grinstead, and Channelsbrook near Horsham, protecting the wealden route to the north.

Next to Bramber came the rape of Lewes, the castle there guarding the wide estuary of the Ouse as well as the ports of Seaford and Newhaven, and Lewes itself. For a time a garrison looked down from a temporary motte erected on the summit of the Caburn. To the east of Lewes lay the rape of Pevensey. Here the Normans utilised the great Roman fortress, building a singularly massive Norman keep against and over the Roman wall. Later in the Middle Ages a moat and inner bailey, incorporating the Norman fortress, were built within the angle of the Roman walls. Pevensey was still an important port. Further to the east came the rape of Hastings. Hastings was already a place of some importance. Like Pevensey it had possessed a mint since the 10th century, and for a brief period in the 12th century it became the most powerful port in the south-east. The harbour lay inland in the river estuary that then separated Hastings from what is now St

Leonard's. The promontory on which the great Norman castle was built stretched some distance out to sea, giving additional protection against storm and tide. Most of this, with the castle, has since crumbled, while the site of the harbour has been built over and paved.

Within twenty years of the Conquest the Domesday Survey of the whole country was carried out, and from this record a fairly clear picture of Sussex at the beginning of the Norman period can be constructed. Unless there were many omissions, settlements seem to have been almost completely confined to the coastal area, the downland, and the greensand belts. On the Weald clay, and in the central Weald, only a few settlements are recorded. It does not necessarily follow that these areas were still uninhabited forest, but rather that any settlements which existed were small farmsteads, or the huts of semi-nomadic charcoal-burners and forest workers. Most of the villages situated along the southern edge of the Weald had extensive pannage rights, that is, the right of feeding pigs on fallen acorns and beech mast, and this is occasionally referred to in the Survey. Such use of the forest would involve huts for the swineherds. Small communities of this kind, however, with little or no area of cultivated ground, and with feudal relationships which could not easily be defined, would not interest the Domesday commissioners.

47 *18th-century drawing of Arundel Castle showing motte and bailey.*

In the area where agricultural communities of a recognisable feudal pattern existed, the largest single group—approximately 6,000 out of 10,000— were classified as villani, or villagers. These had a share in the common fields of the village and owed services and payments of various kinds to the lord of the manor. The size of their holdings might vary from seven to 30 acres. Although the Normans attempted to introduce an element of order and uniformity, in later centuries, when the customs of various Sussex manors were recorded, there was still a surprising variety in the types of payment or service.

Next in number to the villani came the bordars, who formed rather more than one quarter of the population. These had rather smaller holdings but owed similar duties. Below these came a class of cottars, with little land, and maintaining themselves, for the most part, by working for their neighbours. Right at the bottom came the serfs. Of these 420 were recorded, less than one in twenty-five of the population. The serfs held no property in land and were mostly the household servants of the manorial lord. Only 260 persons were listed as burgesses or townsmen, but most of the town dwellers would in fact be villani in status. Few townspeople at that date would be divorced from the land, towns were still only large villages, and the townsman, even though he might be a specialist craftsman, was also a farmer, although he might delegate to others work on the land. The total population enumerated in the Survey is between ten and eleven thousand. Allowing for certain omissions, such as the forest dwellers, the inmates of monastic houses and others, and remembering that those enumerated are the heads of households, which included all generations, grandparents and grandchildren sharing the common hearth, this gives us a total population for Sussex of between sixty and seventy thousand. Although the large towns

48   *Round   tower, Southease*

and coast resorts did not exist in 1066, and a large part of the central Weald was uninhabited (or at least unrecorded in the survey), the population was not so thinly spread in the rest of the County as it might seem at first sight. It is true to say that there are many villages where the population today is smaller than it was in 1066. In the seventh century Bede estimated the Sussex population at seven thousand families, a total population of some forty thousand. This suggests a remarkable stability during four centuries. The Norman Conquest shook Sussex out of this stagnation.

Other significant details of the Domesday Survey include the location of saltpans where sea-water was trapped in shallow basins and evaporated. Two hundred and eighty-five of these are listed, mainly along the river estuaries; a possible site of one of these survives today, in the 'Dripping Pan' on the south side of Lewes. Salt extraction was certainly an important local industry. It was vital to medieval economy, since the salting of meat and fish was the only form of food preservation known, and the lack of root crops for winter feeding resulted in the autumn slaughter of much **49** *Sussex in the* livestock and the salting-down of the winter's meat supply. Watermills— *Domesday Survey* 157 in all—are recorded in a large number of manors. The fisheries were

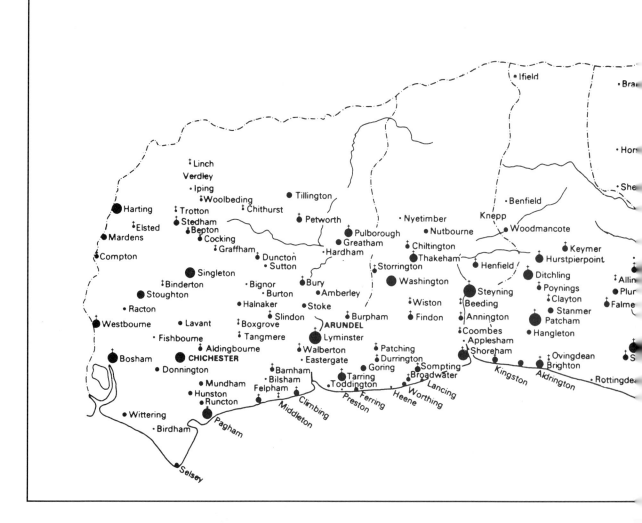

also important at various centres along the coasts. Tenants at Bristelmestune (Brighton), for instance, paid a rent in kind to the lord of the manor of 4,000 herrings—at Southease 38,500! Southease has a church built early in the Norman period with a tall and massive round tower. Both it and others such as those of Piddinghoe and of St Michael's at Lewes, standing at the edge of what was then a wide estuary of the sea, were possibly designed to serve as beacon towers to guide fishing boats to their harbour.

Much local material still remains to be extracted from Domesday Book by careful analysis, and there remain of course many problems and queries. A large number of places, for instance, cannot be identified with certainty, even allowing for considerable change in spelling—places such as Sifelle, Mesewelle or Laneswice.

The map *Sussex in the Domesday Survey* shows the general distribution of population, but we must remember that most of the larger manors, such as Malling near Lewes, Harting, Washington, Patcham, Lyminster and Singleton, included large areas which were not coterminous with the parish or concentrated in the villages bearing these names. In many cases several villages or small hamlets may have been included in one manor, and many

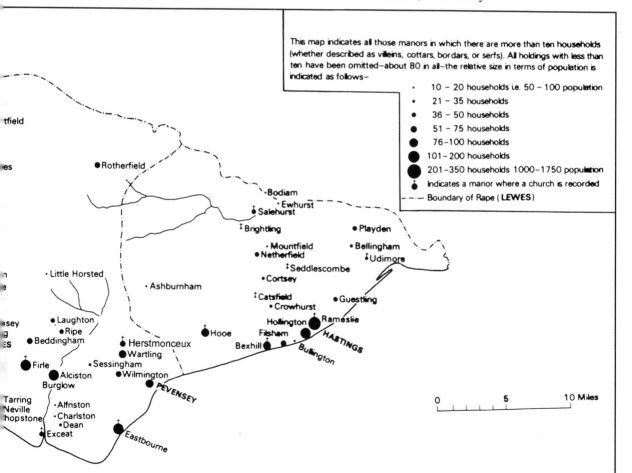

This map indicates all those manors in which there are more than ten households (whether described as villeins, cottars, bordars, or serfs). All holdings with less than ten have been omitted—about 80 in all—the relative size in terms of population is indicated as follows—

- · 10 – 20 households i.e. 50 – 100 population
- · 21 – 35 households
- ● 36 – 50 households
- ● 51 – 75 households
- ● 76 – 100 households
- ● 101 – 200 households
- ● 201 – 350 households 1000 – 1750 population
- ╪ Indicates a manor where a church is recorded
- —·— Boundary of Rape (LEWES)

of these large manors, described in Domesday Book, were subsequently divided into separate manorial holdings or sub-manors. The reverse was also true, namely that occasionally a single village was divided between two, or sometimes three, small manorial holdings.

Eighty-five churches were recorded, but again a reservation needs to be made. There is reason to suppose that the mention of a church was only incidental and that only a small percentage of the churches that existed was in fact noted. In several cases churches which contain undoubted pre-Conquest work, such as Selham, Poling, Arlington, Clayton and Singleton, are not mentioned. Nor are those mentioned necessarily the largest or most important. Finally, most of those mentioned were entirely rebuilt later in the Norman period, since only a few contain work which can be dated before the Survey. Undoubtedly the great majority of churches at the time of the Survey were of wood, their gradual rebuilding in stone being undertaken subsequently.

The map *Norman Sussex* includes most of the more important churches built or rebuilt during the later Norman period, while that on Domesday Book indicates churches actually recorded in the Survey.

50 *Norman Sussex*

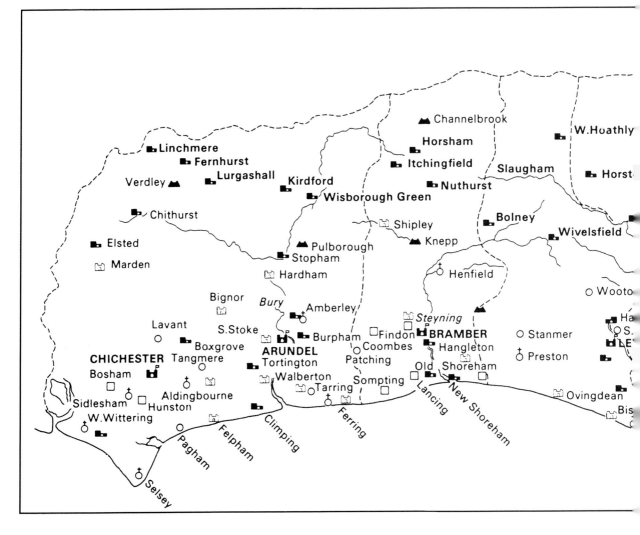

It is in this central Weald that the greatest transformation took place in the century that followed the Domesday Survey. By the close of the 12th century it was studded with thriving settlements, while three new market towns, Midhurst, Horsham and East Grinstead, were sufficiently important by the 13th century to be invited to send representatives to the first Parliaments. The number of churches built, and, in some cases, enlarged before the end of the 12th century, within the area that was still forest in the time of Domesday Book, is also some indication of this development. On the other hand there is little evidence of any extensive revival of iron working before the 13th century, although there is a rather teasing reference in the Domesday Survey to iron-ore working in the Hundred of East Grinstead.

We might have expected that some part of the Weald, which, at the beginning of the Norman period, constituted the largest area of uncleared forest south of the Trent, would have been declared a royal forest. A good deal of Hampshire and Essex was so designated. That this was not done in the case of the Weald was no doubt due to its position across the main routes to Normandy and any application of the Forest Laws to the Weald

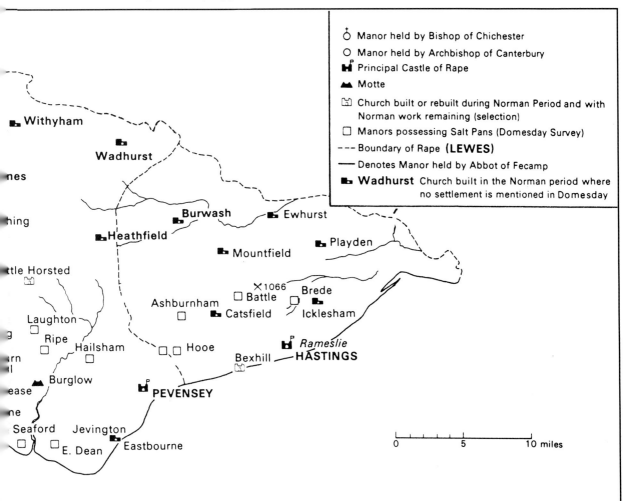

51 *Reconstruction of Worth Church, Saxon style but Norman plan*

would have retarded settlement. Much forest however remained, and local disputes over often ill-defined hunting rights were frequent. In the Middle Ages hunting was not simply a recreation, but an important supplementary source of food. In forested areas hunting rights were therefore jealously guarded. As late as the year 1274 we find, for instance, the Hundreds of Steyning and Poynings reporting the extension by the Earl of Warrenne of rights of 'chase and free warren ... to the great damage of the country who used to enjoy the right' . Close to the main London to Worthing road at Knepp, an isolated ruin can be seen which is all that is left of a hunting lodge forfeited by William de Braose to the Crown in 1066. King John visited the lodge on several occasions. In 1213 he sent his 'keeper of the Hounds, with eighteen keepers, his fellows, and two hundred and twenty of our greyhounds to hunt the does in the park at Knapp'—a sizeable foray!

Elsewhere the overall pattern of village, field and town was little changed except for increasing size, though any kind of exact comparison is impossible since no survey comparable with Domesday Book was undertaken again until the first census in 1801.

Buildings in the Early Middle Ages

After the Norman Conquest an increasing percentage of ordinary dwelling houses were built in stone, and a number have survived in Sussex, though mutilated or in ruins, from the 11th, 12th and 13th centuries; for the latter century there are a few timber-framed buildings still intact which provide both plans and details of construction. These are all houses of manorial or equivalent status, so that we still have nothing above ground to show what the house of the average villager was like. The archaeologist is hampered in discovering what is in the ground by the continuous occupation of sites. We are forced back, therefore, on to such evidence as can be got from an abandoned village such as Hangleton.

One of the smallest cottages among the buildings excavated dates from the 13th century, and has been reconstructed at the Weald and Downland Open Air Museum at Singleton. It gives some idea of what many of the humbler cottages of the Middle Ages may have been like. Below the Downland turf, the walls of this cottage still stood three feet high at one point, and in this corner was an oven sufficiently complete to make possible an exact reconstruction. As the village for six centuries had been given over to sheep pasture, there had been little or no disturbance and the height of these walls could be estimated. They were two feet thick at the base, built of solid flint rubble with lime mortar, tapering slightly to the eaves at about four feet six inches above the ground. The interior space measured 13 by 21 feet, and was divided into two rooms by a wattle and daub partition. In the larger room was a central hearth let in flush with the floor, while the smaller room contained the oven. The roof would almost certainly have been of simple paired rafters, joined together by collars above head level.

In the Weald, where timber was plentiful, such cottages would have been of timber-framed construction with wattle and daub panels, but it is reasonable to suppose that the Hangleton cottages represent in size and

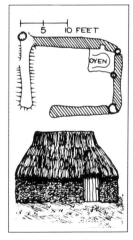

52 *Plan and reconstruction, Hangleton Cottage*

accommodation the kind of dwelling in which the humbler villagers lived. At a time when window glass was beyond the resources of small houses, doors and windows were small to keep out the weather. Shutters or oiled cloth could be put up against wind or rain; how far the latter might be left permanently in position we do not know. After dark, the flames from the wood fire would give some light, and the open areas of the roof provided space for smoke to accumulate and percolate through gablets at each end of the roof. Furniture would be of the simplest kind—a table on trestles or on three legs (the advantage of three legs being that they can adjust to an uneven floor), a bench, one or two three-legged stools, and against the wall there would probably be a chest for storage which could also be used as a seat. For sleeping there might be a truckle bed on wheels which could be pushed out of the way when not in use, or else tiered bunks in a corner of the room—round the hearth and on shelves a few storage pots and cooking vessels and wooden platters and bowls. Such furniture provided the bare necessities for living when life was spent mainly out of doors and centred round the open hearth on winter evenings.

53 Mermaid Street, Rye. This street preserves, with its cobbled stones, much of the flavour of the Middle Ages. Most of the houses on either side, including the Mermaid Inn *(foreground right) are timber framed and date from the 15th and 16th centuries: but many have been concealed by later stucco or brickwork.*

If we assume that this was the kind of very simple one- or two-roomed dwelling of a large part of the population, we can be rather more explicit about the houses of the richer members of the community. There is at Pagham a fragment of a stone house dating almost certainly from the 11th century incorporated in a later building and only revealed during alterations to the latter. This fragment contains a finely cut doorway of Caen stone. The late 12th-century halls of the ecclesiastical manor of Amberley and the Bishop's Palace at Chichester are still intact, incorporated in later additions, and the solar wing of the Archbishop of Canterbury's manor of Tarring still stands virtually as it was built. At Swanbourne, near Lewes, at Lodsworth and in Rye are early 13th-century halls still, though modified, in good repair and in use as dwellings. The basic plans remain the same whether one is dealing with the cottage or the manor house, and whether the materials are stone or timber, namely, a central hall forming the living space with one or more rooms at one or both ends of the hall, and in the larger houses divided into two storeys at these ends. In the larger manor houses there was normally at the end of the hall a parlour, and above this a room usually called the solar. This word seems to have meant simply 'a room high up under the eaves' but gradually acquired the meaning of a rather special room, next to the hall in importance, but not necessarily reserved for any particular purpose. At the other end, called the service end, there would be a buttery and a pantry, and possibly a passage between these leading to an external kitchen. A room over the buttery and pantry would also provide storage space or accommodation. Within this basic scheme there was scope for considerable variety—in size, in relative proportion of one part to another, and in decoration. One can truthfully say that no two medieval houses were alike, and by the 14th and 15th centuries the possibilities of variation were greatly increased in Sussex by the introduction of the jetty.

A few timber-framed buildings survive in Sussex which can with certainty be dated back to the 13th century and, because several of these were originally aisled, it has been argued that an aisled plan, giving greater internal space, may have been usual in the larger timber houses of the early Middle Ages in the county. What does happen in the 13th century is the introduction from across the channel of a quite new technique for supporting adequately the wide roof span; this was the principle of 'crown-post and collar purlin'. One of the earliest and finest examples in the whole of the south-east of England is in St Mary's Hospital, Chichester. The essential feature is the use of massive cambered tie-beams that support at their centre upright posts called 'crown-posts' which in turn support long beams, called 'collar purlins'. These run the whole length of the building, and in turn support the collars which connect each pair of rafters. In Sussex this became, by the 14th century, the most usual form of construction in all the larger houses, as well as in churches and in farm buildings such as barns. The great hall of St Mary's Hospital combines this with aisles and measures nearly forty-five feet in width.

Chichester also has, in the old kitchen of the Bishop's Palace, one of the earliest examples of a method of roof construction which came to be known by the term 'hammer beam'. This was a system of brackets by which the roof timbers could be strengthened and the span increased without either increasing the size of the tiebeam or having recourse to supporting aisle posts. Later it

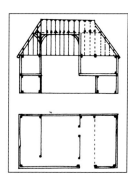

54 *Typical medieval house plan*

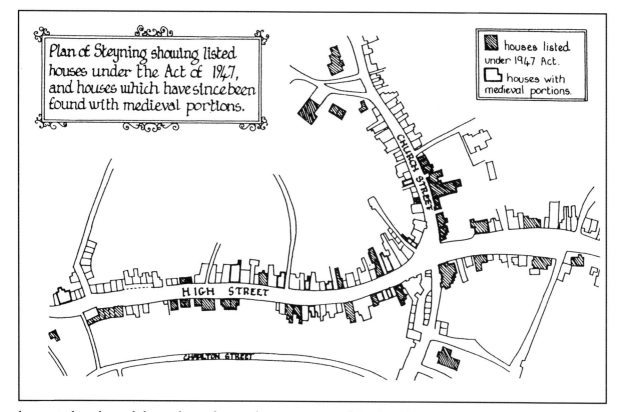

Plan of Steyning showing listed houses under the Act of 1947, and houses which have since been found with medieval portions.

houses listed under 1947 Act.
houses with medieval portions.

CHURCH STREET

HIGH STREET

CHANCTON STREET

began to be adopted throughout the south-eastern part of England in churches, colleges and many of the open halls of the greater houses.

55 *Plan of Steyning, showing listed buildings, drawn in the 1970s.*

In the plans of medieval buildings reference is continually made to a 'bay', and one may speak of a hall of one, two, three or more bays—the bays being the distance between the principal supporting posts. In practice it varies enormously, but has an average approximation to about eight feet. It may owe its origin to the space required for a yoke of oxen, and was derived from the basic unit of agricultural measurement, the rod, pole or perch of five and a half yards, or sixteen and a quarter feet. There is no doubt that the medieval craftsmen were influenced by these standard agricultural measurements when setting out a building, just as a farmer was in setting out his field, but they were regarded as approximations—an average, as it were, to which the individual instance seldom corresponds. In the hall symmetry was seldom observed and the bay at the 'dais' or 'high table' end was almost invariably longer than that of the service end. At the service end, there was usually a passage across the hall from an outside door to another facing it on the opposite side. These doors might be screened from the rest of the hall by a projecting spur or 'spere'.

Part of the difficulty in describing a medieval house is the fact that it is not known for certain how the various rooms were used. Clearly differences of use would depend very largely on the size and status of the house. The search for greater privacy certainly influenced the development of the house, and was one of the main reasons for the revolutionary changes of the Tudor period. It explains the great canopied and screened beds of the 14th century. But, in the smaller houses, life continued close and communal.

Monastic Life

According to Bede, there already existed a small monastery at Bosham when Wilfred converted the South Saxons to Christianity. How long it had been there we do not know: the monks were probably housed in the simplest wooden buildings. At that time the regular monastic plan—church, cloister and communal buildings—was not general. How many other small monastic communities may have existed in Sussex in the two or three centuries that followed we do not know. The foundation at South Malling on the north side of Lewes dates from the eighth century, and there were collegiate churches in the 11th century at Hastings and Steyning. At Hastings the church was partly rebuilt soon after the Conquest, and incorporated within the wall of the castle; that at Steyning was entirely rebuilt on a grand scale a little later.

56 *Monastic Sussex (foundation dates where known)*

These collegiate churches were maintained by groups of clergy leading a semi-monastic life, but engaged in parochial duties. Later such groups were organised under rules akin to those of the Benedictine Order and were

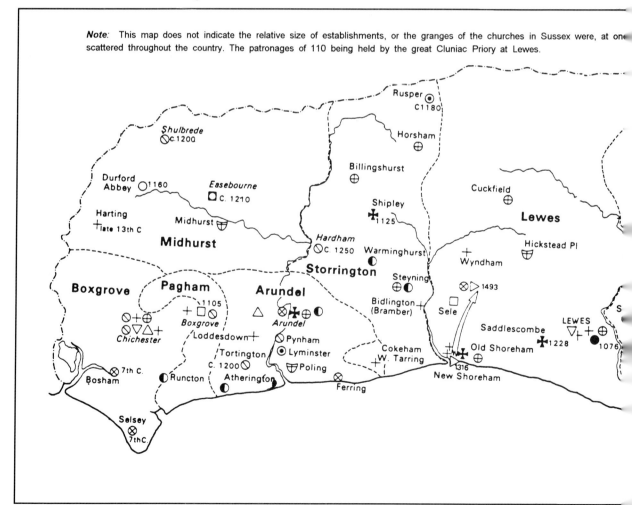

Note: This map does not indicate the relative size of establishments, or the granges of the churches in Sussex were, at one scattered throughout the country. The patronages of 110 being held by the great Cluniac Priory at Lewes.

called Canons. Of these there were two main Orders, the Austin Canons, based on rules originally elaborated by St Augustine, Bishop of Hippo, and the Premonstratensian Canons who followed a later and rather stricter rule based on that of the Cistercian monks.

It was not, however, until after the Norman Conquest that the monastic Orders began to play that vital part in the social and cultural life of the community which was characteristic of the Middle Ages, and which make this period so different in quality from either the centuries before or those that follow. For some fifty years before the Norman invasion, there had been a burst of religious enthusiasm on the Continent. Part of the drive came from the great monastery of Cluny, which by the beginning of the 11th century had some hundreds of daughter houses established in various parts of western Europe. In Normandy this religious revival had taken hold of the population at every level, and found expression in some of the finest buildings of the age; but England, on the whole, lay outside the main current and had been little affected. There was sufficient abuse and slackness in the Saxon church for William to be able to use it as a justification for invasion, and the Norman banners were officially blessed by the Pope before William sailed.

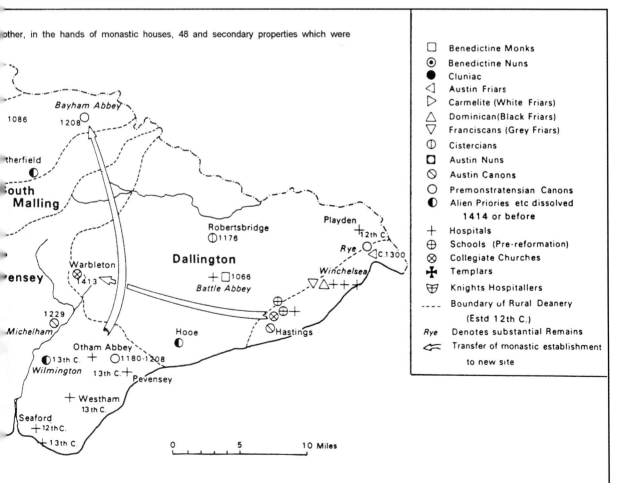

other, in the hands of monastic houses, 48 and secondary properties which were

Bayham Abbey
1086   1208

therfield

South
Malling

Robertsbridge
⬤1176

Playden
12th C.

Rye ⬯ c.1300

Warbleton   Dallington   Winchelsea
⊗1413   ▽△+++

Pensey   +☐1066
                                    Battle Abbey

1229
⬯
Michelham   Hooe   ⬯Hastings
        Otham Abbey   ◑
        ◑13th C. + ⬯1180-1208
Wilmington   13th C.+
                Pevensey

        + Westham
          13th C.

Seaford
  +12thC.
  +13th C.

0   5   10 Miles

☐	Benedictine Monks
⊙	Benedictine Nuns
⬤	Cluniac
◁	Austin Friars
▷	Carmelite (White Friars)
△	Dominican (Black Friars)
▽	Franciscans (Grey Friars)
⊕	Cistercians
⊡	Austin Nuns
⊘	Austin Canons
○	Premonstratensian Canons
◑	Alien Priories etc dissolved 1414 or before
+	Hospitals
⊕	Schools (Pre-reformation)
⊗	Collegiate Churches
✚	Templars
⍕	Knights Hospitallers
----	Boundary of Rural Deanery (Estd 12th C.)
Rye	Denotes substantial Remains
⬳	Transfer of monastic establishment to new site

57 *The restored 14th-century gatehouse to the Benedictine Abbey at Battle.*

58 *Boxgrove. The Benedictine Priory was founded in the early 12th century and was dissolved by King Henry VIII in 1537 leaving only the Priory Church for the villagers to worship in. The ruins of the Priory guesthouse can be seen in the foreground.*

In Sussex the number of new monasteries, hospitals and other foundations established during the hundred years following the Battle of Hastings
is quite astonishing. If we add to this the new churches built and Saxon
churches rebuilt or enlarged, the activity of the Norman masons and their
Saxon apprentices and successors must have been prodigious. The closeness
of contact between Sussex and Normandy is clearly shown in the fact that
stone imported from Caen, the chief Norman port, was used in a great
many buildings within reasonably easy access of the ports and river estuaries.
It was even employed in the House of Austin Canons at Shulbrede in the
heart of the Weald on the Sussex-Surrey border, many miles from the
nearest waterway. This also illustrates how much of the best work went into
the monastic foundations, rather than into the churches, which, although
fine, used only local stone in the inland areas.

A glance at the map will show the wide distribution and variety of the
Norman foundations. In Battle Abbey, and in the Cluniac Priory of St
Pancras at Lewes, Sussex possessed two of the greatest monasteries in the
kingdom. They differed widely both in the character of their administration
and in their contribution to the general life of the community. Battle was
a Benedictine Abbey richly endowed by the Crown, and enjoying special
privileges. Although situated in the forest eight miles from the nearest town,
the enormous guest house suggests that for a time it became a considerable
pilgrimage centre. It soon acquired great wealth, and a prosperous town
grew up under its shadow and protection, while the growing authority and
occasional truculence of its abbots led to many disputes with the feudal
lords of the area.

In contrast, the great Cluniac Priory at Lewes never became a centre of
pilgrimage or a symbol in any way of national consciousness. Founded by
William de Warenne in 1076, it looked to the Continent for inspiration and
leadership—to the network of Cluniac monasteries linked together by
triennial convocations held under the supreme Abbot at Cluny. Although
it was in many ways less a part of the local community, its educational
work and its hospitals were far more important than anything undertaken
at Battle, while its patronage of, and interest in, the arts certainly made a
strong local impact. It is possible that we owe the richness and wide range
of Norman painting which survives in many of the smaller churches in
Sussex to the Priory of St Pancras. They may, in fact, have been done by
a guild of artists based on the Priory. At the Reformation, its attachment
to a wider continental allegiance drew the particular hostility of Thomas
Cromwell, Henry VIII's main agent in the Dissolution of the Monasteries
in 1536 and 1539. He was granted this monastery in recognition of his
services, and had the great church literally razed to the ground; but, by the
irony of fate, he fell from favour and did not live to build the mansion he
had planned for the site. Today the railway runs across the choir and nave
of this church, of which not a fragment stands above ground.

The only Cistercian Abbey in Sussex was founded at Robertsbridge
about the year 1176. The Cistercians followed a more rigorous rule than
any of the other Orders, and deliberately chose what, at the time of its

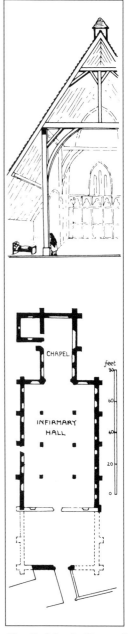

59 *St Mary's Hospital
and plan*

60 *Michelham Priory. The Augustinian Priory was built in 1229. The Priory was defended by a 14th-century gatehouse and what is claimed to be the country's longest waterfilled moat dating from the medieval period.*

61 *The unspoilt interior of the 13th-century church of St Michael, situated in the remote downland hamlet of Up Marden.*

foundation, must have been one of the wildest and remotest areas in the Weald. Little is recorded of its history, but it was one of the three 'Greater Monasteries' in Sussex (the others being those of Battle and St Pancras). These were excluded from the Act of 1536 which closed only the 'lesser monasteries'; yet, at the time of the Dissolution, there were only eight monks at Robertsbridge. Today the size and extent of its buildings can only be judged from crop marks in the fields.

Perhaps the most beautiful fragments of Sussex both in its setting and in its ruins is the Premonstratensian abbey at Bayham, situated at the extreme northern edge of the county. It was founded in 1208 by Canons from an earlier foundation (1180) at Otham near Hailsham. It was built in the severe, early Gothic style favoured by the Cistercians, and a good deal of the church—particularly of the magnificent central crossing, with its simple but soaring lines—survives. Of the only other Premonstratensian house in Sussex—Durford Abbey near Rogate—nothing whatever is left but a few fragments of carved stone and 13th-century encaustic tiling.

Of the smaller establishments, one of the most interesting is the Priory of Wilmington, situated just under the Downs, six miles north-west of Eastbourne. It started as a grange presented by Robert, Count of Mortain, who held the rape of Pevensey, to the Abbey of Grestian in Normandy. By the 13th century it had developed into a small Priory, whose Prior acted as the local agent for the estates held by the mother house in half a dozen English counties. In 1414, at the height of the Hundred Years' War, it was dissolved, with other 'alien' houses attached to French abbeys. It was subsequently converted to a manor house and farm; more of the buildings have survived than is the case with any of the monasteries in Sussex dissolved over a hundred years later. The remains are now vested in the Sussex Archaeological Trust and are open to the public.

The military orders of the Knights Templar and the Knights Hospitaller, founded soon after the First Crusade, established centres in Sussex during the 12th century. In 1115 the Knights Templar were granted the manor and church of Shipley, and later acquired the Church of Sompting (1154), the Manor of Saddlescombe (1228), three miles north of Brighton, and a centre at New Shoreham. In 1312 this great and powerful Order was dissolved by order of the Pope after four years, during which evidence against it was collected by every means available, including the widespread use of torture. In the case of Sussex Templars, the evidence was unconvincing or pure hearsay. It is true that the Templars had become an extremely wealthy and independent organisation, and that their original function had gone with the failure of the last Crusades in the 13th century, but the ruthlessness with which they were finally suppressed by the Pope makes the dissolution of the monasteries 230 years later by Henry VIII seem in comparison relatively humane.

62 *Bayham Abbey*

The lands of the Knights Templar at Shipley and at Shoreham passed, on the dissolution of the Order, to the Knights Hospitaller, whose head-quarters in Sussex was the Preceptory of Poling. The chapel is now incorporated in a dwelling-house, and some of the masonry dates back to the end of the 12th century, but there is no record of the date of its foundation.

Often monasteries were founded with an obligation to perform certain duties for the rest of the community. In the Middle Ages few works were as important as the maintenance of roads and bridges. The Priory of Sele (1080) was responsible for the upkeep of the bridge and causeway across the Adur at Bramber; that of Pynham (often referred to as the Priory of the 'Calceto' or the 'Causeway') was responsible for those across the Arun below Arundel.

Early in the 13th century a new movement—that of the Friars—infused new life into the flagging religious enthusiasm of the later 12th century. Soon after 1225 Franciscan, or Grey, Friars established themselves at Chichester, and after that at Winchelsea and Lewes. Not long after, we find the Dominicans, or Black Friars, also at Chichester and Winchelsea, and at Arundel. By the end of the century, however, the simplicity, sincerity and dedicated quality which had distinguished the early years of the Friars had diminished. The Franciscan church which still stands in the Priory Park at

63 *Fragment from St Pancras Priory*

Chichester has little in common with the simple wooden temporary structures enjoined by St Francis.

Following the Black Death (1347-50), decay both in ideals and practice continued. In Sussex the whole monastic system was in decline: recruitment had become difficult, buildings were falling into ruin and duties went unperformed, while in many cases there had been flagrant local scandals. In 1477 the Prior of Sele was summoned to appear at an enquiry held by the Bishop in the Chapel of St Mary situated on the great stone bridge at Bramber, to answer charges not only of having allowed the bridge to fall into disrepair, but also of virtually embezzling Priory funds in expensive living. In 1478 the Prioress of Easebourne Nunnery, as well as two of her nuns, was accused of gross immorality and of consuming the Priory's resources in hunting and extravagant entertaining.

The tragedy of the Dissolution in Sussex, as in other counties, was that much that was good suffered with the bad. Schools and hospitals maintained by the monastic orders were closed. In Sussex the destruction of actual buildings, both at the time of the Reformation and later, seems to have gone further than in any other counties. We have already mentioned the Cluniac Priory of St Pancras as an example, but more recently many buildings, which survived the initial wave of destruction or adaptation, became quarries for the repair of farm buildings, or were sacrificed for road construction in the 18th century, or stood in the way of the development of agriculture and were razed and ploughed over.

Of the 69 establishments marked on the map on page 58, 41 have completely disappeared and only in 11 is anything substantial left above ground of the domestic buildings. Churches survive in a few cases where they also served the parish, as at Boxgrove, Easebourne: Sele (Beeding) and Wilmington; or were converted to other uses as was that of the Greyfriars at Chichester, and that of the Austin Friars at Rye. Some effort has been made to preserve the remains of domestic buildings, but most are in the hands of private individuals, who have often neither the means nor the will to preserve them. There are, of course, exceptions; for example Wilmington and Michelham Priory, restored and presented to the Sussex Archaeological Trust.

VI *Built in 1330, Lewes Castle barbican,* above left, *still remains in a remarkable state of repair. Particularly impressive are the machicolations and bartizans (the jutting out parapet and turrets from the battlements).*

VII *Some excellent examples of medieval wall painting can be found in Sussex churches, such as at Coombes and Hardham,* above right. *The 11th-century murals in St John the Baptist, Clayton, above the Saxon arch in the nave, are particularly impressive.*

VIII *Arundel is dominated by the castle which holds a commanding position above the River Arun.*

IX *Uppark—a view of the rebuilt house in 1995. Following the disastrous fire in 1989 the restoration work took the National Trust almost six years to complete. The house was built in 1690 and designed by the architect William Talman. It came into the ownership of the Fetherstonhaugh family during the mid-18th century and the grounds were landscaped by Humphry Repton. The National Trust has returned the house to its condition before the fire, using a variety of conservation techniques.*

X *Goodwood House—built by the third Duke of Richmond and designed by James Wyatt at the end of the 18th century. The house and a number of buildings on the estate built at this time contain excellent examples of knapped flintwork. The first Duke of Richmond, attracted to the area by the Charlton Hunt, purchased Goodwood in 1695, which was then a hunting box. Part of this original building was incorporated into the present house.*

7

Chichester and Lewes from the Norman Conquest

Historically and administratively Chichester and Lewes are the most important towns in West and East Sussex. The diocese of Chichester is unique. It has suffered no alteration to its boundaries since the foundation of the Saxon see at Selsey, and it is the only diocese in which an original Saxon kingdom, the see, and the county, have remained coterminous and unaltered since their foundation. The only change is the transfer in 1075 of the bishop's seat from Selsey to Chichester. This reflected a general policy of centralisation, though it was in part dictated by the encroachment of the sea at Selsey. The transfer had an immediate effect in increasing the importance of Chichester. In the Domesday Survey of 1086 Chichester was described as follows: 'In the City of Chichester in the time of King Edward, there were a hundred houses ... and three crofts ... and there are now sixty houses more than there were before.' In other words it had increased by more than sixty per cent in twenty years. It would still be small compared with the Roman city and most of the space enclosed by the walls would be open gardens and crofts, the houses being grouped roughly along the lines of the four original Roman streets which met at the point where the market cross was built later. It was on the site, near to where the Roman forum once stood, that the Norman cathedral was built, probably between 1075 and 1140. A Saxon minster and nunnery is thought already to have occupied part of the site, and, after its demolition to make way for the cathedral, the parishioners were allowed to use a portion of the nave, and later the north transsept for services. In 1187 a disastrous fire destroyed the flat wooden ceiling, the gabled roof, and the clerestory of the Norman building; in the decades that followed these portions were replaced by an early Gothic vault and clerestory, while the original round-ended choir was lengthened, and given a typical English Gothic rectangular east end. Changes and additions were made in the following centuries, including the Lady Chapel and chapter-house at the close of the 13th, additional north and south aisles, the great south transept window and the choir-stalls in the 14th, and spire, cloisters and bell tower in the fifteenth. Apart from these major additions, innumerable minor changes reflect the whole story of the development of Gothic architecture.

The bishop's palace was rebuilt about the same time as the rebuilding of the cathedral after the fire, and the private chapel contains perhaps the most charming example of early Gothic mural painting surviving in this country—a roundel representing the Madonna and Child.

64 *Roundel, Bishop's Palace*

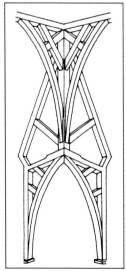

65 *Roof structure, palace kitchen, Chichester*

66 *The Bishop's Palace, Chichester. Between the two projecting wings is an 18th-century screen wall which conceals a 12th-century hall and chapel. The hall itself has been subdivided into a number of rooms. Behind the wing on the right can be seen the roof and the little triangular smoke outlet of the old kitchen. The two wings date from the 16th century.*

Early in the 13th century, while masons were at work restoring the cathedral, both Franciscan and Dominican Friars sought a centre for their work within the city. Later the Franciscans were granted the site of the Norman motte and bailey enclosure within the north-east angle of the city walls. Today only the church which they built (possibly the chancel of a yet larger building) survives. After the dissolution it served as a Guildhall, then as an assize court and, finally and most appropriately, it has been converted into a local museum. Of the Dominican, or Black Friars, whose Priory was situated within the south-east sector of the city, not a trace remains.

There were at least three hospitals; that of St James, founded early in the 12th century for lepers, was well outside the city walls to the east. A fragment of this still survives as a dwelling-house. Another, that of St Mary's built towards the end of the 13th century, is the best example in this country of the usual type of general purpose hospital of the period—a great open hall with beds along each side, and a chapel separated from this by a screen at the eastern end. Though the interior has been modified by the building-in of chimneys and apartments, the essential features remain.

The bishop himself, apart from his palace in Chichester, held various manors in the county directly from the Crown. In days when travel was slow and often difficult, they served as centres from which the bishop on his visitations and journeys through his diocese could be entertained or hold local conferences. Different manors became at different times the favourite residences of particular bishops—Amberley, for instance, was used by Bishop Rede, who added the great hall, now ruined, and in 1377 the surrounding castellated wall; Cakeham, at Wittering, was chosen by Bishop Sherburne, who at the beginning of the 16th century added a lookout tower in early brick. The Archbishop of Canterbury also held some manors in Sussex. One of the largest and most favoured residences was at Mayfield where some of the buildings, including the great hall, have been restored in the present century and now form part of a seminary.

It is impossible within the limits of a brief history such as this to deal with the careers and characters of the many outstanding men who served as bishops of the See of Chichester, but something must be said about St Richard of Wyke, whose tomb in the cathedral became in the 14th and 15th centuries an object of pilgrimage rivalling Battle to the east and Glastonbury to the west. St Richard, rather than St Wilfred, came to be regarded as the patron saint of Sussex. This brought considerable wealth and trade to the city.

St Richard was born at Droitwich in Worcestershire, the son of an independent farmer, and went to Oxford as a poor scholar to study canon law. From thence he went to Bologna, returning to England to become chancellor of the diocese of Canterbury, and a close friend of Edmund, the Archbishop. From Saxon times onwards there had been, at various periods, resentment of the tendency within the medieval Catholic Church to treat England as an outlying province in a clerical empire centred mainly on Italy and France—a province providing convenient emoluments for promising continental clerics, and a source of revenue. This provoked a counter-movement in England, and tension of this kind had been growing during the period of Edmund's archbishopric. On the death of Edmund, Richard continued to oppose papal policy in this matter but his position was complicated when he became involved in a conflict of a rather different kind with the King. In 1244 the Canons of Chichester elected, under royal pressure, a favourite of the King, Robert Passilew, but an enquiry into the candidate's fitness proved that he was utterly unsuited for the office. In his stead the Canons chose Richard. The King refused to recognise the appointment, withheld all the manors on which his income depended, and for two years Richard carried out his duties as Bishop vitually penniless—relying on the hospitality of the parish clergy while visiting and administering the diocese. In 1246 the King relented, and seven years later Richard died at Dover, on his way to France to take part in the organisation of one of the last crusades. He was canonised 14 years later, and in 1276 his remains were transferred to the newly-erected shrine in Chichester Cathedral.

From then on he became one of the most popular saints in the English Calendar. Like St Thomas of Canterbury he symbolised to the ordinary people the triumph of spiritual power measured against the secular, of passive resistance successfully defying the armed power of the State. This division between Church and State, between the spiritual and the temporal, was fundamental to the medieval consciousness, and the Middle Ages cannot be understood unless we are fully alive to it. Certainly the interests of Church and State often coincided, but the division of authority was quite real, and the conflicts and tensions this produced were a stimulus to thought,

67 *Remains of St James's Hospital, and inscription*

and to an integrity of character, which is typical of the period. It is not surprising that one of the first acts of the Reformation, when Henry VIII was declared Head of the English Church, was the ruthless and utter destruction of the shrines of St Thomas and of St Richard. We cannot even be certain today of the spot where that of St Richard stood. Yet for two centuries Chichester had prospered as a pilgrimage centre: so great were the crowds from the villages of Sussex who came on his Feast Day, 3 April, carrying banners and occasionally fighting for precedence, that special officers had to be appointed to order the processions and preserve the peace.

One of the last pre-Reformation additions to the city was that of the market cross. This was the gift of Bishop Storey in 1501, and the Deed of Gift reads: 'To the Sucoure and Comfort of the Poore Peple there ... a Crosse sett and founded yn the midde of the said cite ... no housez shoppez nor stallez to be bilded ... nigh adjoynyng ... to the lett or dist'baunce of the poore peple to sell their chafer there ...' More lies behind this gift than appears on the surface, for it established a market free from restrictions. As early as 1135 the Merchant Guild in Chichester received a charter which confirmed 'All its Ancient Rights', aud in the next century Chichester was declared a Staple, which virtually gave it a monopoly of the wool trade in this part of the country. Such a Guild exercised powers greater than those of a City Corporation today; particularly in economic matters these were usually restrictive. Throughout the Middle Ages an uneasy balance of influence and control in the city existed between the Guild and the ecclesiastical authorities. With the Reformation the balance shifted finally to the citizens, and it is perhaps symbolic that the Guild, then reconstituted as the Guild of St George, acquired the church of the dissolved Grey Friars as their Guildhall. A century later, we find the city divided along these lines, with most of the burgesses supporting William Cawley, a wealthy brewer and benefactor, who had endowed the Cawley Alms Houses in Broyle Road, while the cathedral chapter and clergy supported the Crown.

During the siege of the city in 1642 the suburb of St Pancras on the east side was destroyed. This almost put an end to a local industry of some importance—needle-making. Yet, in spite of all this, Chichester grew slowly but steadily during the next two centuries. At the time of the Civil War the male population of eighteen years or over was 772, from which we can assume a total of perhaps 3,000. (Today the population residing actually within the line of the walls is somewhat less.) In 1801 the population had risen to approximately 5,000; in 1901, 9,000, and in 1991, 25,000. This expansion has been entirely outside the old walls: within the walls, Chichester has preserved much of the proportion and balance of the medieval city, with its central focus of cross and cathedral. But the houses then were of wood. So many were rebuilt or refaçaded in the 18th century that it can rightly be described today as a 'Georgian City'.

During this period Chichester prospered. The livestock market was recorded at the turn of the 19th century as the largest in the country after Smithfield, due probably to its close proximity to Portsmouth and the need to supply the Navy during the Napoleonic Wars. Many fine examples of

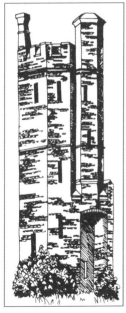

68 *Brick tower, Cakeham Manor*

Georgian domestic and public architecture can be found not only in the main streets but also in St Martin's Square and the Pallants. The Pallants, found in the south-east quadrant, reflect in miniature the city's main street plan. Pallant House, built in 1712 at the end of Queen Anne's reign by Henry 'Lisbon' Peckham, a wine merchant, has been restored as an historic house and art gallery open to the public.

The city continued to be an important market centre throughout the 19th century, but it was not until this century that Chichester experienced its greatest changes, with the building of County Hall just before the Second World War, and continued urban growth in the post-war years as it has strived to cope with the ever increasing problems of motor transport and a growing population. At the same time it has become one of the most important cultural centres in Southern England with its internationally known Festival Theatre, opened in 1962.

Lewes, unlike Chichester has no Roman origins. A Saxon settlement existed at the time of the Conquest and its strategic importance was recognised by William the Conqueror who granted the rape of Lewes to William de Warenne, who built the castle. He also founded with his wife Gundrada in 1076 the great Cluniac Priory of St Pancras at Southover. De Warenne and his wife were buried in the priory, but during the 12th century they were re-interred in St John's Church, Southover.

During the middle ages, Lewes like Chichester had a Merchant Guild and was an important market centre. The town also played a significant rôle in the Barons Wars and, as a result, parliamentary history. In 1264 Simon de Montfort defeated King Henry III's troops at the Battle of Lewes, fought on a site below Mount Harry, near the racecourse. King Henry's headquarters were in the Priory of St Pancras and it was here that the signing of the Mise of Lewes took place. The treaty laid the foundation for what is considered to be the country's first democratic parliament which met in 1265.

69 An early 19th-century market-day scene in East Street, Chichester. The fortnightly livestock or 'beast' market was held in the main streets until 1870. In the background stands the market cross which remained the site of the produce market until 1808.

70 *Portrait of St Richard, Norwich Cathedral*

The formidable barbican at the entrance to the castle was built during the early 14th century. It is an excellent example of medieval military architecture but, by the middle part of the century, the last of the de Warenne's had died and thereafter it lost its importance and gradually fell into disrepair. The castle is now owned by the Sussex Archaeological Society which also owns Anne of Cleves House in Southover, which was granted to Henry VIII's fourth wife as part of her divorce settlement in 1538, although she never lived there.

Following the dissolution of the Priory, Lewes became embroiled in the religious persecutions of the Tudor period. During the reign of Queen Mary, 17 people were burned at the stake in the High Street between 1555-57 for their protestant beliefs. The anti-papist feelings that continued into the 17th century, during these turbulent political and religious times, are still remembered today, when 5 November is celebrated by the various Lewes Bonfire Societies.

Lewes was staunchly Parliamentarian, but did not experience any hostilities during the English Civil War. During the 18th century, Thomas Paine, the political reformer who wrote *The Rights of Man*, lived in Lewes before emigrating to America.

Lewes, like Chichester, prospered during the Georgian period. Many of the town's buildings were built in the style of the day using brick, stone and flint; or the original timber-frame was re-façaded such as at Barbican House, now the headquarters of Sussex Archaeological Society. Thomas Read Kemp, whose name was to become associated with the development of Kemp Town in Brighton during the Regency period, was born here in 1782. Shelleys, now a hotel, is another good example of a former Tudor building being refurbished at this time. Lewes possesses some fine examples of an architectural feature of the 18th century—the use of mathematical or 'M' tiles which were hung onto timber frames to give the mock appearance of their being bricked.

The town was also at this time an important agricultural centre with its market and sheep fair—the pioneering work of John Ellman took place at the nearby Glynde Estate. His development of the local breeds of Southdown sheep and Sussex cattle brought him national recognition. The late 18th century saw the canalisation of the Ouse and the improvement of Newhaven harbour. The assize court and county gaol were at Lewes.

It was a Lewes physician, Dr. Richard Russell, whose prescribing of seawater as a medicinal cure transformed neighbouring Brighton from an insignificant fishing village into a fashionable watering place. As a result of its proximity to Brighton, Lewes was often visited by the Prince Regent and other members of his family and Georgian Society, primarily for the Races.

In 1801 the town's population was 4,909, in 1901 it had risen to 11,249 and in 1991, 15,376. The 19th century saw the growth of business, such as the Russell and Bromley shoe shops chain, Harvey's Brewery and the printing works of William Baxter. But it is as an administrative and judicial centre that its importance is paramount today.

8

Towns and Villages of Sussex
in the later Middle Ages

By the 13th century the medieval pattern of settlement of village and town was complete, but within this general pattern considerable development and readjustment were to take place in the later medieval period. The early part of the century found Sussex at the height of its prosperity. Hastings, which had been a foundation member of the Confederation of the Five—or 'Cinque'—Ports, had become its headquarters in the 12th century, while the Confederation itself had been enlarged by the addition of 'The Two Ancient Towns' of Old Winchelsea and Rye. Thus the dynamic leadership had shifted from the Kentish to the Sussex ports. The Confederation also included among its 27 'associate' members such important Sussex ports as Seaford, with its harbour on the estuary of the Ouse, which then entered the sea close to the town. The export and import inventories of cargoes included goods of every description but the chief exports were certainly timber and wool, while the principal imports were cloth and wine. In the 15th century salt is mentioned increasingly often as an import—an indication that the saltpans, so plentiful in the earlier period, were becoming unworkable.

71 *The town and harbour of New Shoreham was built by the Normans and became, during the Middle Ages, the most important port on the south coast. Charles II sailed from Shoreham in 1651, when escaping from England after his defeat at the Battle of Worcester.*

Outside the Confederation, ports such as Shoreham, Arundel and Chichester were all thriving commercial centres, while inland the pack-horse trade with, and through, the interior of the county had expanded steadily. We have seen how the Weald itself had been largely settled, and flourishing market towns established at East Grinstead, Horsham and Midhurst. Each of these towns was sufficiently important to be required to send representatives to Parliament in the latter half of the 13th century. Thirteen towns in Sussex were represented in these Parliaments as against six for Surrey, eight for Kent, 12 for Hampshire, and approximately 200 for the whole country. The pattern of representation established then became fixed in the following centuries, and it is some measure of the later decline of the maritime boroughs that Camden in 1586 writes of Shoreham, Bramber and Steyning: 'The commodiousness of the Haven by reason of banks and bars of sand cast up at the river's mouth has quite gone: whereas in fore-going times it was wont to carry ships with full sail as far as Bramber, which is a good way from the sea ..., a little from this lieth Steyning, once a great market and at certain times and set days much frequented.' Of Hastings he writes: 'The tradition is that the old town of Hastings is swal-lowed up by the sea. That which standeth now is couched between a high cliff to seaward and as high a hill landward ... the haven, such as it is being fed but with a poor, small rill is at the south end of the town'; and of Rye: 'It beginneth to complain that the sea abandonneth it ... and that the river Rother loseth his force to carry away the sands and beach which the sea doth invite into the haven.' Three hundred years, however, before Camden, and long before their final decline, the ports of Sussex were given a terrible warning, had they been able to interpret the signs, in the destruction of Old Winchelsea.

72 *Plan of New Winchelsea*

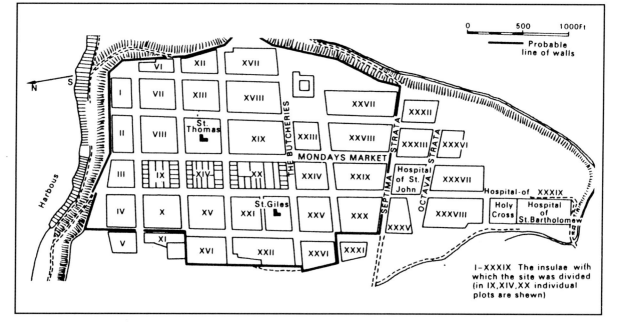

Old Winchelsea had been built on a low-lying island, in what was then the wide estuary of the East Sussex Rother. It rose rapidly to importance, and early in the 13th century had supplanted Hastings as the most influential member of the League, when disaster overtook it. It is just possible that the unprecedented storms, which at intervals battered and destroyed walls and houses, were aggravated by a slow rise in the sea-level. In 1250 the town lost 300 houses, and in 1252 the Chronicler Matthew Paris wrote: 'At Winchelsea, a place extremely important to the English, and especially to the Londoners, there was a great inundation, the sea submerging mills and houses, and drowning a large number of the inhabitants.' Plans were already in hand to resite and rebuild the depopulated and half-ruined town on the adjacent mainland, when an even more violent storm in 1287 finally swept it out of existence. So complete has been its obliteration, that it is impossible to say exactly where Old Winchelsea stood. Yet there was evidently no clear understanding of either the natural forces which were slowly but inexorably altering the character of harbours and anchorages, or of the probable importance of Sussex in the changing trade routes of the 14th and 15th centuries: for it was planned to rebuild Winchelsea on the grandest scale. The town was never completed. Although the streets were laid out and the walls and gates built before the wharves and warehouses below the walls on the north side had all been constructed, the anchorage was already found to be inadequate in depth, and dredging to be impracticable. Today lush meadows cover the area planned as the harbour.

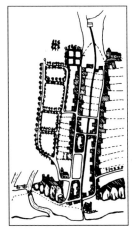

73 *Plan of Hastings, 1741*

At Rye the process was slower. As late as the 18th century there was still a fairly wide anchorage immediately adjacent to the walls, while an 18th-century map of Hastings still indicates a diminutive harbour where the main centre of the town stands today.

The most important industry of Sussex was undoubtedly shipbuilding. The shipwrights were able to draw from the oak of the Weald, which was generally recognised as providing the finest timber in Europe. The iron industry which had existed in the Weald in Celtic and Roman times had been revived, particularly in the area round Battle, and in the Worth and Tilgate forest areas round Crawley. In the north-west corner of the Weald, in the area between Kirdford and the Surrey border, a glass-making industry had been established some time in the 12th or early 13th century. Its centre was just across the Surrey border round Chiddingfold. Like the iron industry, it depended on the suitable conjunction of raw materials—in this case (apart from timber for fuel) the right quality of sand, and large areas of bracken, which was cut green and burnt for the production of potash, which served as flux. In 1240 Laurence Vitrearius was given the contract of the stained glass windows at the east end of the abbey at Winchester, and in 1352 John de Alemagne for those in the Royal Chapel of St Stephen. Such contracts indicate the prestige of this wealden industry, while the French and German names associated with it are the beginning of a long succession of immigrant continental craftsmen, who, particularly in the Tudor period of continental religious persecution, settled in Sussex, revitalising other industries including those of iron and clothmaking.

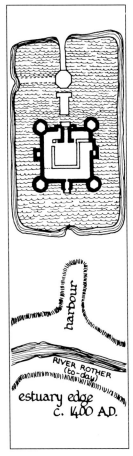

74 *Plan of Bodiam Castle*

75 *Steyning has some excellent examples of medieval timber-framed buildings, particularly in the High Street and Church Street. In this photograph, The Grammar School, the brick built building to the left, was founded in 1614. The house to the right is a good example of a 'Wealden' house.*

In all this we are witnessing a shift of emphasis from the coast to the Weald, and it is not unreasonable to assume that many of those who found employment in the timber, the glass or the iron industries may have been descended from once prosperous burghers of Shoreham, Hastings or Winchelsea. Another indication of this shift in the relative importance of the Sussex towns can be seen in the location of pre-Reformation Grammar Schools other than those already established in the boroughs. They are at Cuckfield, Battle and Billingshurst, all within the Weald—two in the heart of the iron area, the third on the edge of the glassmaking district.

The period from the end of the 12th to the middle of the 14th century was one of great building activity. More churches were rebuilt or extended in the early Gothic style than in the style of any other period. The principal Norman castles were enlarged, and manor houses were rebuilt in more spacious and convenient form, often in stone. Two of the finest castles in the county (Bodiam and Herstmonceux) belong to the last phase of the Middle Ages. Bodiam was built in 1385 by Sir Edward Dalyngrigge, a veteran of the Hundred Years' War with France. It was designed as a second line of defence in the event of a French invasion. Rye at the mouth of the eastern Rother had already been sacked in a French raid eight years previously, and Bodiam commanded the upper reaches of the Rother estuary which was even at that date still a quarter of a mile wide where it flowed past the castle. The plan of the castle was itself influenced by French models. As a purely defensive structure (before the development of effective siege cannon) it was one of the most perfectly designed castles in the kingdom.

Still later, towards the close of the Hundred Years' War, the castle of Herstmonceux was built by Sir Roger de Fiennes (another veteran of the war), between 1440 and 1447. As at Bodiam, one motive was certainly defence against a French landing on the flat Pevensey levels which the castle commands. Like Bodiam, it was inspired by continental models—in this case the use of brick was copied from the Flanders region. Herstmonceux was in fact the first building of any size to be built of this material in England since Roman times. Flemish brickmakers and bricklayers had to be brought over to supervise the work.

76 *Brick turret, Herst-monceux*

Some of the changes that took place in the later Middle Ages, such as the decay of the Sussex ports or the decline of the monasteries, were undoubtedly hastened by the universal calamity of the Black Death. This is particularly true of the countryside. In the village communities from the coast to the edge of the Weald Clay the pattern of life established in the Saxon period had continued with little change up to the 14th century. Perhaps the effect of the Black Death can best be illustrated from the records of one typical manor, that of Wiston at the foot of Chanctonbury.

For centuries the management and life of this manor had followed the routine laid down in its custumal, which fortunately has survived. The following entry indicates how exactly the obligations of every tenant were defined: 'Henry Calwe holds 1 ferling of land and gives of rent yearly at the feast of St Thomas the Apostle 8d, and at the feast of the Nativity of St John the Baptist 8d, and to the Sheriff's Aid 2d, and to Parksilver 1d. And he shall give at the feast of St Thomas the Apostle 1 cock and 1 hen and at Easter 5 eggs. And he ought to work from the feast of St Michael to the feast of St Peter ad Vincula [1 Aug.] in every week 1 [day's] work, except the 3 weeks at the Nativity of the Lord and at Easter and at Pentecost. And he ought to do from the feast of St Peter ad Vincula to the feast of St Michael 16 works [days' work]. And he ought to reap, bind and carry to the lord's grange half an acre of wheat for 1 work ...' and so on for more than two pages. What was required in 1 (day's) work was, it will be seen, defined exactly, and whether Henry Calwe did it in person, or whether it took him five hours or fifteen hours was not the lord's concern, provided it was done. The contract was exact and explicit and everyone knew where he was.

This particular custumal dates from the early years of the 14th century, yet within a couple of generations the picture had completely changed. Between the years 1349 and 1352 more than half of the tenants had died from the Black Death, their holdings lay vacant and, what was vital from the lord's point of view, the general economy of the manor, as an estate, was jeopardised since the due services were not forthcoming. The resulting competition between manorial lords for such labour as was available led to the rapid substitution of rent and wages in place of the traditional services and payments in kind. Generally speaking, the effect of the Black Death in Sussex was the break-up of the village community as it had existed from early Saxon times. The enclosure by voluntary consent between the tenants of the open fields seems to have been largely completed by the Tudor period, unlike some of the midland counties, where they survived almost intact into the 18th century. These changes led to the decentralisation of the old compact village. Tenants now paying rent in lieu of service rebuilt their

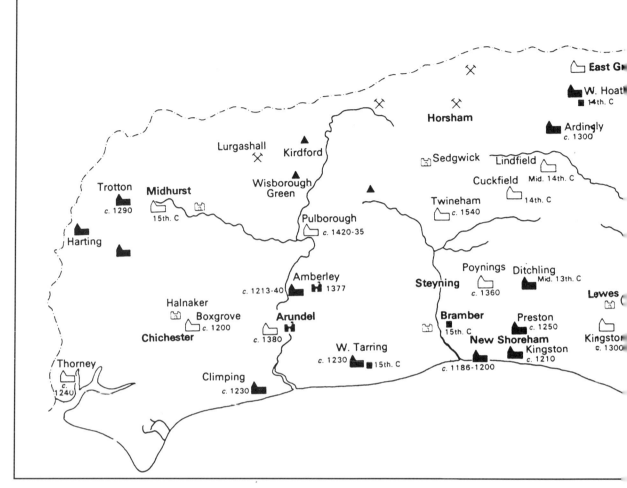

East G◥

W. Hoat▮
14th. C

Ardingly
c. 1300

Horsham

Lurgashall
Kirdford

Sedgwick
Lindfield

Cuckfield Mid. 14th. C
14th. C

Trotton
c. 1290

Midhurst
15th. C

Wisborough
Green

Twineham
c. 1540

Harting

Pulborough
c. 1420-35

Poynings
Ditchling
Mid. 13th. C

Amberley
c. 1213-40   1377

Steyning

Lewes

Halnaker
Boxgrove
c. 1200

Arundel
c. 1380

Bramber
15th. C

Preston
c. 1250

Kingston
c. 1300

Chichester

New Shoreham
Kingston
c. 1210

Thorney
c.
1240

W. Tarring
c. 1230   15th. C

Climping
c. 1230

c. 1186-1200

77 *Medieval Sussex* houses within their new holdings. The church, previously the focus of the village, often became stranded in open country. In the downland area, where sheep farming had always formed an important element in manorial economy, the lord of the manor was able to make up for vacant holdings by an extension of grazing, and, in some cases, the village ceased to exist as at Hangleton above Brighton, or Barpham above Worthing.

Building Styles

One building, and only one, dominated the village in the Middle Ages— the church. The manor house might be, and often was, close to the church, and also the priest's house, but, relatively, these were unimportant. The church was the symbol of community. The great phase of rebuilding in Sussex during the 13th century was partly the result of continuing prosperity and population expansion, partly a reflection of a new religious consciousness.

In the 14th and 15th centuries the picture is rather different. Churches were not so frequently rebuilt or enlarged. In some areas, as in the Adur valley, from Bramber to New Shoreham, churches actually fell into decay. In other places improvements rather than extensions of space were made,

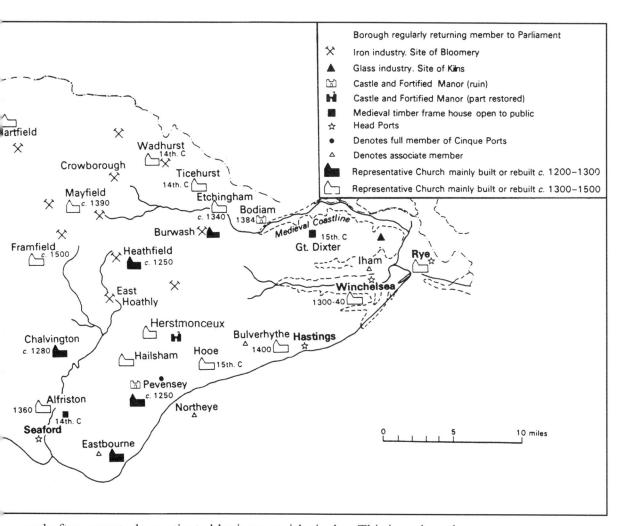

and often seem to be motivated by inter-parish rivalry. This is perhaps best seen in the building of bell towers to house the more impressive peals of bells now fashionable. For example, the neighbouring parishes of Cowfold, Henfield, Thakeham and Washington all added towers within a few decades of each other. Only in a few cases were churches completely rebuilt— Poynings, Etchingham and Arundel, towards the end of the 14th century, Pulborough, with the exception of the chancel, in the 15th century—the first three mainly at the charge of the lord of the manor, the fourth through a legacy from its priest. Compared with East Anglia or the West Country, church building in Sussex in the later Middle Ages was relatively modest and reflects its relative decline compared with these other parts of the country. In the towns the differences are still more evident. The decay of the churches of Steyning, Shoreham and New Winchelsea are striking testimonies to the declining population. Following the sack and burning of Hastings by the French in 1337 only two of the previously existing seven churches were rebuilt. Although the churches of Sussex lack the richness of late medieval work found in some other counties of England there is still a great deal of late English Gothic to be found in the form of minor improvements, such as inserted windows.

The county is fairly rich in commemorative tombs and tablets, and is one of the first in which the technique of commemorative brasses was introduced from the continent. The early 14th-century brass of Margaret Camoys in Trotton Church is probably the finest surviving early brass in England, and those of the Gage family at Firle some of the best from the late 16th century.

It is surprising that in a county so rich in timber and with a fine tradition in timber domestic building, there are relatively few late medieval roofs, screens or other forms of decorative wood carving comparable with those of Somerset or any of the East Anglian counties. Two timber-framed churches survived into the 19th century—at Plaistow and at Loxwood. Both are recorded in the collection of drawings made between 1781 and 1783 for Sir William Burrell's projected history of Sussex. The one at Loxwood, dating from the 14th century, was replaced as late as 1898.

It is a different story when we turn to the houses of the period. Only a few houses, apart, that is, from castles and the larger manors, can be dated back to the 13th century, and most of these are stone built; but by the 14th century there are many, particularly among the farmhouses in the Weald. In this region there appears to have been a continuous improvement and rebuilding of farmsteads both before and after the Black Death. This supports the view that the tendency towards more compact and more efficiently run farms took place earlier in the Weald than in the rest of the county, although the large number surviving may also be partly due to the more plentiful supply of timber resulting in more substantial and more durable buildings.

In timber-framing the most striking development, both in design and technique in the later Middle Ages, was the jetty. It increased enormously the possibility of variations in design. The jettying of one storey over the one below was, of course, only practicable in a timber structure. It certainly had a practical advantage in towns where the saving of space was important, and where the jettied upper storeys would give some protection from the weather to those using the narrow ways which separated the two sides of the street; and it was almost certainly in London that jettying first became a general practice. From there fashion and prestige would be likely to spread the idea quickly in the Home Counties, whether it served any practical purpose or not.

In Sussex the earliest jettied buildings date from the 14th century. Apart from the emulation of town by country, which was operative then as now, there must also have been appreciation of the scope which the jetty gave for new and interesting experiments in design: before the end of the century there had developed in the Weald an adaptation of the jetty which created one of the most attractive forms of timber building that has ever been conceived— the 'Wealden' house. In the 15th century it became widely distributed throughout the Weald, spreading into the Downland, and as far as Hampshire to the west. In the 'Wealden' house the problem of combining a jettied upper floor with the open hall, the walls of which must rise straight from foundations to eaves, was solved by recessing the hall between the projecting upper floor rooms at each end of the hall. By carrying the roof across the recess by means

78 *The Preacher's House, Ewhurst. The continuous jetty became very popular in the Tudor period. The timber framing of the upper floor is concealed by tile hanging. The close studding of the ground floor, however, is well preserved. The brick oasthouses and the weatherboarding contribute to a group typical of the north-eastern*

79 *The Priest House, West Hoathly. Built around 1400, this house is a good example of the unjettied type of open hall. The chimney was inserted and the wall divided horizontally and vertically towards the end of the 16th century.*

80 *St Mary's, Bramber, incorporating the surviving wing of a late 15th-century courtyard inn. A good example of the use of close set vertical timbers (known as 'close studding'), a fashion which became widespread in Sussex at that time.*

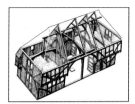

81 *Diagram of a 'Wealden' house*

of a massive eaveplate, supported by brackets, it was possible to incorporate the jettied wings and the recessed hall under one continuous roof. Although this may seem a simple and straightforward way of solving the problem, it did involve quite complicated structural details.

These 'Wealden' houses represent perhaps the finest expression of medieval house design for that intermediate section of the population lying somewhere between the lesser nobility and the ordinary peasant or villager; most appear to have been built by the rising class of yeoman farmers and by successful traders and craftsmen in the larger villages and market towns. More than any other form of medieval building they have suffered from constant alteration which conceals completely their original appearance, usually by incorporating the hall recess and the space beneath the jetties by a new façade. A survey in Robertsbridge revealed the existence of eight 'Wealden' houses, some quite fragmentary, but four of remarkably fine quality. In a survey of four in Steyning, that which became the Poor House retained its external appearance, one had been divided into two cottages and the others converted into shops.

An interesting feature of these 'Wealden' houses is that the interior dimension of the hall usually approximates to a cube. This is partly because there was structural weakness if the hall recess was increased in length beyond a certain point. These dimensions give a surprisingly dignified, spacious quality to the interior. The proportions of brackets, posts, tie-beams and other details, were carefully judged and not dictated simply by questions of stability and strength.

Many houses of traditional design were being built or rebuilt during this period. A few very small halls, with width as little as 11 or 12 feet, have been found and may represent the dwellings of the new copyhold class now free from the servile restrictions of villeinhood. A number of priest's houses survive, from the tiny hall at Itchingfield to the manor-house proportions of those at West Hoathly and the ancient Prior's at Crawley, or the finely decorated hall of the rectory at Sutton and the massively built Old Rectory at Burwash which was demolished in 1969.

In many of the market towns there would have been inns with closed courtyards. One side of what was almost certainly an inn can be seen in St Mary's, Bramber, a house open to the public. This stood at the end of the great stone bridge over Bramber Water. Built towards the end of the 15th century, it was attached to the priory of Sele which had the responsibility of maintaining the bridge and the chapel which stood midway across the bridge. What is left appears to be the east wing of what was once a large enclosed courtyard with arched entries for the passing of carts which could with their drivers be accommodated within the court. Both the *Mermaid* and the *Flushing* inns at Rye, portions of which go back to the 15th century, and the cellars of both to the 13th century, were probably of this type, as was the *Great George* inn at Petworth, which was demolished last century.

Many towns would have had market halls. These were usually in the form of a council chamber or guild hall over a lower, open arcade where traders might have stalls. If they were timber-framed the upper storey was frequently jettied on all sides. The stone-built market cross at Chichester provides only an arcade shelter—but at Midhurst a fine timber-framed example with two storeys above the arcade still survives, though very much modified. Others at Petworth and Horsham are recorded in late 18th-century drawings, made before their replacement in the early 19th century by the present stone-built town halls. Their original purpose required a central position, and few could withstand the changing needs of trade and traffic in the 19th century.

For the same reason the medieval style of shop disappeared, but at a much earlier date. With its horizontal 'counter' projecting into the street and its unglazed opening above which the craftsmen could be seen at work, few survived even into the 18th century. During demolition in 1968 of a shop in the centre of Horsham a Victorian pseudo-timber-frame concealed a genuine medieval town house and shop. This consisted of three storeys, both the first and the second floor being jettied, so that the original gable would have projected some five feet over the street. It had three rooms, one above the other, but behind these three rooms was another bay open from the ground to the rafters, providing an enormous open recess to serve as a chimney bay to the shop on the ground floor. This presumably formed the general working area.

82 *The market hall, Midhurst, built around 1520, preserves some herringbone brick in-filling—an early example of this use of brick.*

The continuous terrace may also have been more frequent in towns than has hitherto been supposed. Part of such a terrace of four can be seen in the old cottages at Tarring, preserved by the Sussex Archaeological Society. Built in the late 15th century they were of a form sometimes described as 'modified Wealden' in which, although the hall was recessed, the roof is continued over the jetty at one side only, the other side being built as a separate wing at right-angles, with the gable end facing the street. An analogous terrace of the same period but in stone can be seen in the Vicars' Close at Chichester. Originally this was twice its present size with a facing terrace enclosing a long central garden area—a kind of modified cloister. The courtyard plan derived from Rome runs like a theme with variations through the medieval scene. Excavations at Arundel of the site of the Maison Dieu—a mixture of alms house and hospital founded in 1395—has shown this to have been a large courtyard, quite unlike the completely centralised plan of the great aisled hall of St Mary's Hospital at Chichester.

83 *14th-century doorway, Priest House, West Hoathly*

These few surviving examples of types of medieval building help us to visualise something of the Sussex village and townscape towards the close of the Middle Ages in, say, the decade before the dissolution of the monasteries; but it is still necessary to bear in mind the limited extent of our knowledge. Of the smaller houses and cottages in which most people lived, very little remains, and about the general appearance of the buildings there are a number of uncertainties. It is known, for example, that limewash was very widely used as a disinfectant and cleanser both for external and for internal walls, and in the case of timber-framed buildings (and these formed the majority in Sussex), was often applied not only over the wattle and daub infill but over the timber frame as well. The blackening of the timber frame is a much later fashion, and the medieval village did not necessarily present the magpie black and white contrasts which please the 20th century. There were even local bye laws stipulating that thatch should be regularly covered with a coat of lime as some precaution against fire. Where such bye laws were actually enforced, many villages and farm groups would have had an external appearance unlike anything to be found today outside certain places in Wales, where it is possible to find slate roofs whitened as well as walls.

Another uncertainty is roof covering. Broadly speaking, in Sussex thatch was probably used in the main corn growing areas for most buildings including many of the churches. Clay tiles were, however, used much more generally than is often supposed, particularly in the north and eastern parts of the county, while along the coast the excavations at Hangleton suggest that stone slates imported from Cornwall or Brittany were to be found even on some of the smaller houses. In the central Weald the laminated sandstone sometimes known as 'Horsham slab' was widely used as roofing in the larger houses and buildings. There are many references to shingles in Sussex medieval accounts, and it is clear that wooden slats or shingles, probably of cleft oak, were widely used.

Perhaps there are two things at the beginning of the 16th century that should strike the observer from the 20th century most forcibly, the complete absence of glass in windows, which were mostly small in size and positioned on the north and east rather than the south and west, and, except for a few town houses, the complete absence of chimneys, though the use of ornamental coverings to the smoke outlet in the roof may have been more usual and more elaborate than often supposed. It is in these features particularly that revolutionary changes begin to take place within the next half century.

9

Sussex in the 16th and early 17th centuries

Great Mansions

Perhaps the most striking evidence of the shift in the economic and social life of Sussex at the close of the Middle Ages from the coast to the Weald is to be found in the large numbers of country mansions built during the late Tudor and Stuart periods. These are almost all confined to the area north of the Downs. A great deal of this building is linked with the expansion of the iron industry, manor houses being rebuilt or enlarged from profits derived from the sale of timber, or from shares in the new iron foundries. One or two important mansions such as Rowfant, near Crawley, were built by iron masters; others, such as Slaugham and Wiston, were built by families greatly enriched by the industry. Yet others were built by the new class of rich merchants from London, who wished to set themselves up as country gentlemen—a process which has continued ever since. An excellent example of this is the manor of Woolavington, which was purchased in the reign of Elizabeth by Giles Garton, citizen and ironmonger of London. He greatly enlarged and rebuilt the manor house. A most interesting plan and contract made between Garton and Henry Hobbs, mason of Arundel, survives, and is probably fairly typical of the building contract general in those days.

The contract, dated 1586, specified that all the stone was to be provided by the mason, but Garton was responsible for 'lyme, brycke, sande and nayles ... spades, bucketts, also scaffold bordes, poles, hurdles, also all flynte, chawke ... also pyble stones and gravell for roughe costinge of the same ...' Payment was to be made gradually as the work proceeded, and the last paragraph of the contract reads: 'Fynallye the saide Henry is contented and doth covenant ... that if any of the saide stone buyldinges after the setting upp of the same shall by wynde, weather, rayne or otherwise be decayed or for wante of his good workemanshippe then he ... shall upon requeste to him ... forthwith at his costes and charges repaire and amend well and substanciallie all suche the decayes and defaultes duringe the space of one wholl yeare nexte after the finishings of the same worke.' This house was entirely rebuilt towards the end of the 18th century, but the fine Tudor walled garden, with corner gazebos in moulded brick, still survives.

Other mansions were built by the growing body of important civil servants, lawyers and placemen, a class which proliferated during the Tudor period. Many of these had been rewarded by substantial transfers of monastic land

and building after the dissolution of the monasteries. Of the two richest prizes in Sussex, Lewes Priory and Battle Abbey, the first was granted to Thomas Cromwell; the second, Battle, to Sir Anthony Browne, Standard Bearer of England and Lieutenant of the Royal Forests. Sir Anthony razed to the ground church, cloisters and chapter-house and built a magnificent mansion on the site from the materials of the Abbey. His half brother, William FitzWilliam, Treasurer of the King's Household, acquired the Priories of Shulbrede and Easebourne, and the Abbey of Durford near Midhurst, and, having purchased the Manor of Cowdray, built there the most splendid of all the Tudor mansions of Sussex.

Cowdray was typical, though on a grander scale, of what happened in the case of some dozens of other mansions in the county. The original residence, which first gave protection and encouragement to the growing market town of Midhurst, was the Norman castle of Savaric de Bohun on St Anne's hill, which overlooks the town. In the 14th century the site was abandoned for a more comfortable, if less strategically defensible, site in the meadow to the north, at the edge of a wood called Le Coudreye. This formed a nucleus for the great mansion to be built nearly two centuries later. In 1528 Sir David Owen, who by marriage had succeeded to the de Bohun estates, sold the property to Sir William FitzWilliam, who completely reconstructed the manor. In 1543 Sir Wiliam died without issue, and the property passed to his half-brother, Sir Anthony Browne. The main building was virtually completed by the end of the reign of Henry VIII, but additions, such as the tall oriel window of the Hall—one of the earliest exploitations

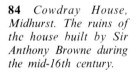

84 *Cowdray House, Midhurst. The ruins of the house built by Sir Anthony Browne during the mid-16th century.*

of glass on a large scale in a domestic building—and the great staircase were made a little later. One of the most interesting features of the house consisted of piped water, which was gravity-fed from a pump-house on higher ground some two hundred yards to the north of the mansion. Although in 1793 the house was completely gutted by fire, some surviving details, such as the fan-vault in the entrance porch of the Hall, together with the drawings which were made shortly before the fire by the artist Grimm, indicate that the quality of the craftsmanship and the richness of the decorative detail were equal to the best produced in this period anywhere in England.

In more than one way such country houses replaced the monastic establishments of the previous centuries. Although they were entirely secular in their ideals and organisation, and provided few of the services, whether in education, care of the sick, or hospitality, which had been important functions of the monasteries at their best, they nevertheless did become the real cultural centres in the life of this country during the next three hundred years. Music and the arts were patronised, and perhaps flourished by reason of their divorce from the limitations of ecclesiastical control. The greater houses kept open house more effectively than many of the monasteries. The pageants and feasts organised in their halls and grounds were usually shared by the whole community in much the same way as the religious festivals had been. At Cowdray an important officer was the almoner. Another element common to both was the strict ordering and discipline of the establishment, and the paternal conception of the duties of the lord and steward to the community. A book of rules for the household compiled in 1595 by the second Viscount Montague, grandson of the first Sir Anthony Browne, survives, giving some idea of the way in which these great houses were managed during their heyday.

The duties of 37 principal household officers and servants are set down in detail. Of the almoner he says:

I will that the Almoner, while he is within the Hall, be at the direction of the Usher thereof ... that he keep it clean and swept with boughs and flowers ... I will that he make the fires within the Hall when the fire is there to be used, namely, from All Hallowes Eve at night to Good Friday morning. That he cover the tables when the dishes are laid forth for them ... that he attend to fetch beer, bread and other necessaries for the gentlemen waiters ... that he preserve the broken meats, bread and beer for the poor; that he distribute the alms considerately with due regard and respect to the poorest and the most needy: and to conclude that he keep his place at meals with the gentlemen servants and see that table to be well ordered.

Of the steward he writes:

The choice of an officer in so high authority shall be such that I will make small doubt of his commendable carriage of himself in his face according to the great trust that I repose in him ... will that he do customably dine and sup in the Hall, and that always in gown unless he be booted for honour or order's sake ... I will that in civil sort he do reprehend and conect the negligent and disordered persons, and reform them by his grave admonition and vigilant eye over them: the riotous, the contentious and quarrellous persons of any degree, the revengers of their own injuries, the privy mutiners, the frequenters of tabling, carding, dicing in corners and at untimely hours and seasons, the conveyors of meat and other matters out of my house, the hunters of ale houses, or suspicious places by day, or by night ... I will that he do convent apart and after some admonition at his discretion, upon due proof, restrain and forbid their attendance upon me until myself shall otherwise determine.

Considering the laxity and irresponsibility which had invaded so many of the monastic establishments in their later years, it is perhaps somewhat sentimental to assume that the change was necessarily for the worse. It is impossible to forgive the destruction of buildings, libraries and works of art, but these new mansions were at least well maintained, and the estates efficiently managed.

Cowdray belongs to the early and middle years of the 16th century. Parham and Wiston, within a few miles of each other, provide an interesting comparison at the century's close. Both were 14th-century manor houses, rebuilt between 1588 and 1600; the hall at Wiston has a double hammer-beam roof—one of the last open halls of the medieval form to be built in the south of England, while that at Parham, with its flat, decorated plaster ceiling and panelled walls, reflects the Renaissance influences, then beginning to dominate Tudor architecture.

85 *Mansions: selective list*

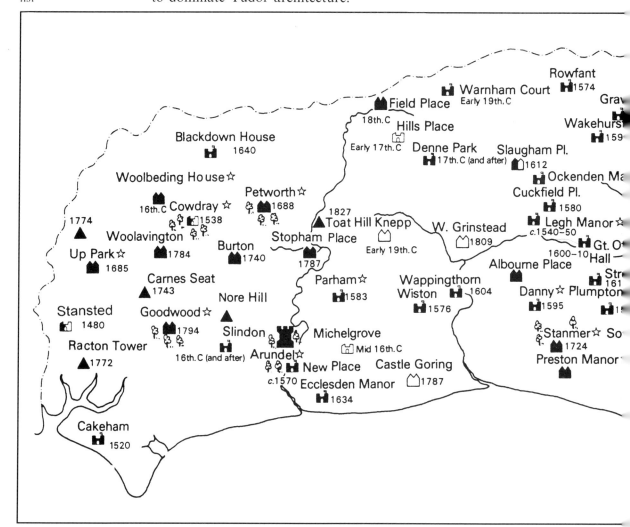

Several of the houses which today present the typical Elizabethan E-shape façade were originally much larger. Wakehurst, Cuckfield Place and Wiston all enclosed central courts, as at Cowdray, and occupied as much as twice their present area, before being reconstructed in the 18th and 19th centuries. Other mansions were reduced both in status and in size, as at New Place, Angmering, which is now divided into three cottages.

Danny, near Poynings, Legh Manor near Cuckfield, and Bolebroke, near Hartfield, are three of the few remaining mansions built entirely of brick during the late Tudor period in Sussex. Many of the stone-built houses incorporated brick in the chimneys, wall linings and for other details in the manner employed at Cowdray; but it is, perhaps, significant that three of those houses which were the first to be built entirely of brick in the early Tudor period—Buckhurst near Withyam, Michelgrove near Findon, and Laughton Place near Firle—were all later demolished.

One of the last mansions to be built of timber in Sussex was the Ote Hall at Wivelsfield in 1612. By then, timber for building was already in short supply, thanks to the iron and glass industries: hence brick began, of necessity, to be increasingly used for every type of building during the 17th century.

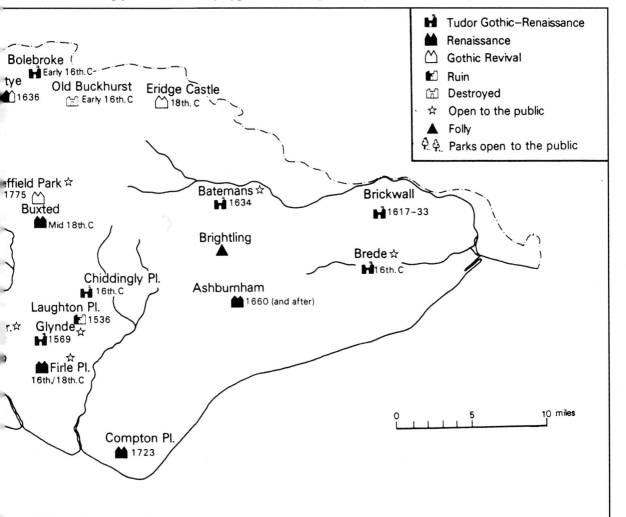

86 *Hammer beam roof, Wiston House.*

This was practicable almost everywhere in Sussex since good clays for brickmaking are very widely distributed.

The 17th century is not quite so rich in greater mansions as the 16th, but a word must be said of two—Slaugham Place, built at the beginning of the century, and Petworth House at its close. Slaugham Place, like Cowdray, is now a ruin, though for a different reason—the abandonment of a house too large to support, a fate not confined to the present age. Slaugham is of particular interest as one of the first fully Renaissance-style mansions both in plan and in much of its detail. Unlike Cowdray, Petworth and most of the other great houses, it did not incorporate any part of an earlier building. It was built in 1612 by Sir Walter Covert, one of the most respected figures in Parliament throughout the reign of Elizabeth and for many years 'Father of the House'. In the middle of the 18th century the Covert family household at Slaugham is recorded as numbering 70, yet before the end of the century the house was a ruin and much of the stone was sold for roadmaking. Today the remains of the house, except for two fine, arched arcades, are overgrown, but the surrounding walled garden, with a raised terrace at one side, and charming gazebos at each corner and in the middle of the longer side, is the most complete surviving example in Sussex of this early style of garden planning.

Petworth House, like Cowdray, incorporates part of the earlier house, in this case the 13th-century chapel, and is possibly the fourth rebuilding on the same site. Although the side facing the park to the west is a balanced Renaissance design, the rest of the exterior is singularly untidy: an attempt was made in the 18th century to reface the remainder of the house, but only the southern end was completed. Both Petworth, and another fine house of the same period, Up Park—near Midhurst—were presented to the National Trust. Although many great mansions were built during the last two hundred and fifty years—Sheffield Park, Goodwood and Warnham Court to name only three—they do not compare in quantity, quality or variety with those of the 16th and 17th centuries.

From Open Hall to Inglenook

The gradual step-by-step character of the revolution, or rather evolution, in house plan and design from the medieval to the modern and the disappearance of the open hall with its central hearth did not happen all at once: there was a period, roughly that of the 16th century, which can rightly be called 'transitional'. Towards the end of the 15th century the central hall was becoming smaller in relation to the rooms at either end, with the hearth moved towards the lower end, and the building of a canopy to direct the smoke away from the rest of the hall. The next logical step was to use the space, now clear of smoke, more efficiently by inserting a floor. Within the lower end, now a 'chimney-bay', the hearth remained open although a funnel-like canopy constructed of timber frame with wattle and daub infilling might direct the smoke to a louvre or outlet in the roof.

A recent survey of one Sussex parish revealed at least two houses in which a sequence of four successive changes, spread possibly over three or four generations, could be traced before the final insertion of a brick chimney breast and inglenook.

More significantly, a number of houses have been found which were designed and built to conform to particular stages in the process of change; halls for example with large canopied smoke-bays built at one end.

When these gave place to brick, or, more often, a combination of stone and brick chimney breasts, these were built so that they still could provide sufficient space to sit on either side of the hearth. Inglenooks of this kind, even in relatively small houses, were sometimes as much as 12 feet across and over three feet deep, and small cottages, numbers of which survive with little alteration, were provided with inglenooks. They were taken as much for granted by the end of the 16th century as the open hearth had been in the Middle Ages. A couple of centuries later the majority of these inglenooks were bricked up or converted into cupboards with small grates substituted, as coal gradually took the place of wood.

Windows, however, remained small, and for the most part unglazed. Glass, although general in the greater mansions, was relatively expensive, and a glazed casement remained a luxury to the majority of the population well into the 17th century.

Compared with the medieval open hall, the ground floor rooms of the 16th-century houses with their low ceilings must have seemed small and very cosy. It is just possible that a contributing factor was climatic. The period covered by the Tudors and the early Stuarts has been called the 'little ice age', and there certainly appears to have been some worsening of the climate compared with the earlier Middle Ages.

Accompanying these changes was the rapid spread of the use of brick. By the middle of the 16th century, brick was in use not merely for the new chimney breasts, but began to take the place of wattle and daub for the infill of timber-framed buildings. Brick was also being combined with wattle and daub and stone and flint, and its use for corners and the jambs of windows and door openings enabled rough stone, as well as flint, to be used more effectively. Quite early in the 16th century it was also being used for the entire fabric of every type and quality of building, including churches such as those at Twineham and East Guldeford, and it was not considered inappropriate to use it for additions to existing churches as at Egdean, Burton, Warminghurst, Ford and many others. There is no doubt that shortage of timber was a principal cause. Not only was the population in general steadily increasing but the growth of London was phenomenal, and London depended on the timber of the Weald and the Home Counties for most of its buildings, its shipyards and fuel. At the same time the consumption of timber by the iron and glass furnaces was also increasing.

The activity which must have existed within the wealden area of Sussex, before the replacement of timber by other materials, is impressive. The amount of labour that must have been continually employed in sawpits, in carpenters' and builders' yards, providing timber for houses, ships, barns, waggons, furniture and farm equipment as well as the subsidiary employments of servicing the woodlands—felling and transporting—must have been huge.

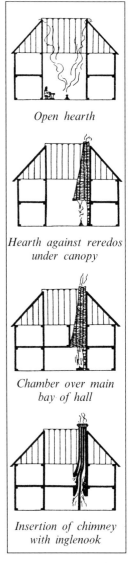

Open hearth

Hearth against reredos under canopy

Chamber over main bay of hall

Insertion of chimney with inglenook

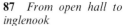

87 *From open hall to inglenook*

Other innovations during this period which affected the interior and external planning and appearance of houses include the introduction of the dormer window, which had been long in use on the continent. These made it possible to utilise the space within the roof, provided a floor was inserted and an access stair. In towns this would be valuable, but by the end of the 16th century attics with dormers are found even in quite rural cottages. New buildings were now more often of three storeys and this was not confined to the towns. Quite unsuspected examples were recently uncovered in Horsham and in East Grinstead, one during demolition, the other during its reconstruction.

The 'semi-detached' paired cottages became increasingly general later in the 18th and 19th centuries, but whereas more recent examples were almost always minor versions of each other, identical in every way, those of the 16th and 17th centuries were more frequently disparate. Often one is slightly larger, with better mouldings and more convenient stairs, or a more commodious inglenook, such as six timber-framed paired cottages in the small village of Houghton. It seems that the deliberate avoidance, characteristic of the Middle Ages, of mechanical repetition was still motivating the craftsmen of the early 17th century—an attitude quite different from that which lies behind the precisely paired estate cottages of the 18th or 19th centuries or of a rebuilt and replanned village such as Milton Abbas in Dorset.

Much evidence has been accumulated of widespread freehand interior mural decoration, mostly dating from the middle of the 16th to the first half of the 17th century. Such decorations usually were painted in black on a lime plaster surface, and in some cases the design was carried over timber-framing. In several examples the entire surface of all four walls was evidently decorated; and some paintings have been found in polychrome. These painted rooms are normally on the upper floor: with the abandonment of the open hall this floor seems to have taken on the importance, almost, of hall and solar.

88 *Mid-16th-century town house, Midhurst*

The Sussex Iron Industry

In Celtic, Roman and medieval times iron smelting was carried on in various parts of the Weald, but, up to the end of the 15th century, it had been a relatively small-scale industry based on a simple furnace, in which charcoal and iron ore were built up in layers to form a circular mound, perhaps three or four feet high, over a central stone hearth. This was then encased in clay and ignited, air being forced in by bellows at the base. It took two or three days to burn through, and at the end a certain amount of semi-molten 'plastic iron' was formed on the hearth at the base of the mound. This could then be beaten out, cut and shaped in a forge. The lumps of iron were called 'blooms'. A single bloomery produced a small amount of iron at fairly long intervals, and the work could be carried on by one or two families with the help of perhaps an equal number of charcoal burners and iron-ore miners. Not more than a few hundred persons would have been engaged at any one time in the industry.

Towards the end of the 15th century a revolution in the technique of smelting was made by iron workers in the forest area of the Ardennes in northern France, and from there the new technique was introduced into the Weald. The first furnace and hammer forge in the country was established at the end of the 15th century at Newbridge in Ashdown Forest. It involved the building of a permanent structure with a large furnace chamber and a wide chimney. Into the furnace chamber projected a number of great bellows; these, compressed one after another by a rotating wheel which could be driven by water power, oxen or horses, forced air continuously through the furnace chamber; the mixed charcoal and ore burned not only more quickly but at a much higher temperature so that the iron became completely liquified and could be run off from the base of the chamber into moulds. The furnace was fed from the top and therefore could be maintained almost indefinitely. A large blast furnace could produce as much iron as twenty or perhaps thirty bloomeries. This improvement coincided with an increased demand for iron for the production of heavy cannon, which could now be made in moulds, instead of being built up of bands of iron, as were the primitive 'crackys' or 'culverins' first used at Bannockburn (1314) and Crécy (1346). In addition, there was an expanding market abroad for these new and improved engines of war. The difference between the banded cannon from Eridge made of wrought iron strips bound together with iron hoops and the great cast iron guns of the 16th century represents not merely a revolution in the methods of war, but a revolution in technology.

89 *A cut-away illustration of a 17th-century Wealden water-powered charcoal blast furnace at North Park Ironworks, Fernhurst, showing the bellows arch and casting arch. The furnace was used for the production of cannon.*

90 *Charcoal provided the fuel for the iron industry, particularly during the 16th and 17th centuries. Charcoal burning has continued to be carried out in Sussex and today there is a small revival in the craft to supply the barbeque market. The traditional method using an earth kiln, shown above at the Weald and Downland Open Air Museum, took approximately three days and two nights to burn and a six cordwood kiln could produce about one and a half tons of charcoal.*

The Sussex Weald was admirably fitted for the rapid development of the iron industry along these new lines. It contained sufficient supplies of excellent iron ore, mostly in layers at the base of the Wadhurst Clay, and very large areas of timber for fuel. Soon a transformation of the Weald took place which attracted national concern. A Royal Commission was set up in 1573 and reported: 'Besides these furnaces aforesaid, there are not so few as a hundred furnaces and Iron Mylles in Sussex, Surrey and Kent, which is greatlie to the decaie, spoile and overthrowe of woods and principle tymber, with a great decaye also of tillage for that they are continuallie employed in carrying of furniture for the said workes, and likewise a great decaie of the highways because they carrie all the wintertyme.'

In 1574 the Privy Council obliged all makers of cannon to enter into bonds not to manufacture or sell without licence from the Queen. In 1581 an Act was passed to check the destruction of timber near London, and prohibited its conversion into fuel for the making of iron within 14 miles of the Thames while forbidding the erection of new iron works within 22 miles of London. Such restrictions no doubt encouraged developments in Sussex, but another Act restricted the cutting of timber within 12 miles of the coast, in order to protect the shipbuilding industry of the Cinque Ports. Other restrictive Acts were passed in the years that followed, but were evidently ineffective since the industry continued to expand. In 1607 John Norden in his *Surveyor's Dialogue* wrote: 'He that well observes it, and hath known the Weald of Surrey, Sussex and Kent, the grand nursery of oak and beech, shall find an alteration within less than thirty years as may well strike a fear lest few years more as pestilent as the former will leave few good trees standing in those wealds. Such a heat issueth out of the many Forges and Furnaces for the making of iron, and out of the glass kilns as hath devoured many famous woods within the wealds.'

In the north-west of the county the situation was aggravated by the expansion of the glass industry. As in the iron industry the introduction of new techniques, in this case by Huguenot glass-workers from France, had been responsible. One of these, Jean Carrée, built a large furnace at Farnefold Wood near Wisborough in 1567. Many other furnaces in the Kirdford, Petworth, Loxwood area followed—one was discovered as far south as Graffham. One of the best examples of a charcoal blast furnace has been excavated at Northpark Ironworks, Fernhurst. For a time therefore there was, in this part of Sussex, keen competition between the iron master and the glass-workers for the available fuel supply, and in 1615 an Act was passed prohibiting the further use of wood fuel for glass-making—a triumph for the iron interests!

91 *Cast-iron fireback, Lewes Martyrs*

Ultimately the rapid expansion of the iron industry ensured its equally speedy extinction. The available forests of the Weald were literally swallowed up by the furnaces. As early as 1547 the accounts of the ironworks at Worth record the consumption during the two previous years of nearly 6,000 cords of wood for the furnace and of nearly 3,000 for the forge—a cord being about two tons of wood. Other factors contributed; many furnaces controlled by families loyal to Charles I were disbanded or destroyed by Parliament in the Civil War. Finally the discovery of methods of coking coal, so that coke could be used in place of charcoal, led to the migration of the industry to the Midlands and the North. By 1717 only 20 furnaces were still active in the Sussex Weald, and only seven in Kent and Surrey combined. In 1809 the last furnace—at Ashburnham—drew its fires for the last time.

92 *Glass furnace, 16th-century drawing*

It is difficult today to realise the enormous change in the wealden landscape that these hectic years of industrial development involved. The clearing of much of the Weald in Norman and later medieval times had been relatively slow and unspectacular; while the areas specifically reserved as woodland, had been carefully tended by those concerned, whether lords of the manor, burgesses, or individual farmers. The system of 'coppice and standard', by which selected oaks were encouraged to grow by adequate spacing, had ensured timber for the building of both houses and ships. There had been continual trade with London and the larger towns, including as we have seen a valuable export trade with the continent. Instead of these carefully husbanded forests, there was now a barren wilderness. Quick and immediate profits had led to a lack of concern for the future. There was little or no replanting at the time. Dotted among the now barren hills and valleys were dozens of lakes, artificially created by dams to provide water power for the hammers and bellows, or washing facilities for cleansing the ore. Today, surrounded by pleasant woods, these form part of the attraction of the Weald. But this

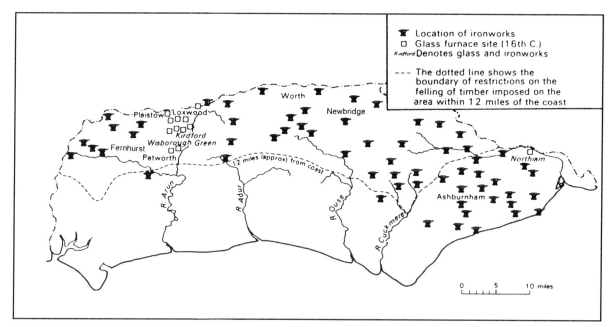

93 *Iron and Glass Industry, 16th-17th centuries*

is only one side of the picture; the thousands who had been attracted as labourers when the industry was at its height were now without employment, and a period of distress followed which certainly contributed to the reckless and desperate character of some of the smuggling gangs.

Another consequence was the ruination of the roads. There is no reason to believe that travelling in medieval Sussex was particularly difficult or that the roads were bad; by the 17th century they had become notorious. As early as 1585 an Act was passed to compel the iron-masters to contribute to the roads which they used. The Act provided that, for every six loads of charcoal or ton of iron carried, one cartload of 'sinder, gravell, stone, sande, or chalke' should be laid on the highways and that the Justices of the Peace were to see that this was done. This Act seems to have been ineffective and unenforceable, but it is the first attempt to make the user contribute, in proportion to his use, to the cost of maintenance. It is the amplification of this principle, in the first Turnpike Act in 1663, which led directly to the Turnpike System which revolutionised road transport in the 18th century.

There was much in the Sussex iron industry of the 16th and 17th centuries which foreshadowed the industrial revolution of the 18th. The new blast furnaces were in part financed by capital provided by London merchants, the landowners receiving shares in the product in return for land and timber concessions—an early form of Joint Stock enterprise. The industry was also dependent on a supply of free mobile labour, and certainly recruited a great part of its labour force from the landless proletariat created by enclosures during the Tudor period in other parts of England. It is one of the paradoxes of history that the earliest large-scale manifestation of those developments, which became the basis of the later industrial revolution, should have occurred in this now rural residential county.

10

The Civil War and Nonconformity

The cannon foundries of Sussex had an important rôle to play in the struggle between King and Parliament, but it was not only this which made the control of Sussex of vital importance, and led to a series of campaigns which, although not decisive, played their part in determining the ultimate outcome of the Civil War. Sussex and Kent lay on the shortest route to France and, although the ports were in decline the kind of assistance which Charles hoped to receive from France—bullion and arms—could be more easily smuggled across the Channel to the shores of Sussex than to any other part of the south coast. For these two reasons, therefore, it was necessary for Parliament to prevent the Royalists gaining control of the county.

As in many other parts of England it is impossible to make any clear distinction of class or location between those who supported the Crown and those who supported Parliament. Among the gentry, families were often divided cousin against cousin, occasionally brother against brother. Although the majority of the older families supported Charles, a considerable number supported Parliament. The following is an extract from a letter by the Royalist Sir William Campion of Danny (near Ditchling), to his great friend, Colonel Morley of Glynde, principal leader of Parliament in Sussex.

94 *Cawley almshouses, Chichester*

> I did not rashly or unadvisedly put myself upon this service, for it was daily in my prayers for two or three months together to God to direct mee in the right way ... I believe that you think not that I fight for Popery, God knows my heart, I abhor it. God Prosper me no further than my desires and endeavours tend to the preservation of the Protestant religion settled in Queen Elizabeth's days, the just prerogative of the King, and just privilege of Parliament. However, I heartily thank you for your desire of the preservation of mee and mine, and if ever it lie in my power to do any courtesy to you, it shall not be wanting in your faithful friend and servant.

Such a letter typifies the character of the conflict and the heart-searching it provoked in all who were involved. Of the 59 signatories to the death warrant of Charles I, seven were Sussex men, three of them great landowners. In the countryside attitudes were very often determined by identification with—or hostility towards—the local great family.

In the towns it is singularly difficult to trace any general pattern. Of the 13 boroughs returning members to Parliament, five were divided, three had both members supporting the Crown, five had both members supporting Parliament. It might have been thought that the coastal boroughs would at least have felt strongly about the justice of levying ship-money from inland

95 *West Gate, Chichester, 1781*

counties towards the maintenance of sea defences. In fact only Hastings was strongly Royalist. The strange atmosphere of the early months of the conflict was vividly illustrated in Chichester. From the day when the King raised his banner at Nottingham on 22 August 1642, to the first local engagement on 15 November, when the gentry from the surrounding area entered the city and gained temporary control of it by surprise, supporters of both sides had been drilling daily in different parts of the city, almost within a stone's throw of each other—the Royalists in the Palace precincts, the Parliamentarians in the north-east sector. Chichester was in fact more clearly divided in its loyalties than most of the other towns. The clergy were almost entirely for Charles, and the bulk of the burgesses for Parliament.

The action taken by Parliament on the news of the seizure of Chichester indicates how seriously the control of Sussex was regarded. A large force of 6,000 men was immediately dispatched under General Waller to retake the city. At the same time a subsidiary force made a detour to Arundel to reduce what was, potentially, the strongest fortified centre in Royalist hands: but which, at the time, was garrisoned by only 100 men. Arundel Castle fell almost immediately: Chichester held out for six days, during which the suburb of St Pancras on the east side was almost entirely destroyed by fire. Eventually a breach was made through a bricked-up gate which had been cut through the city wall at the bottom of the deanery garden some two centuries earlier. In the days which followed some damage was done to the fittings of the cathedral by zealots to whom music, stained glass and other imagery was synonymous with popery; but this can be exaggerated, and was little compared with the systematic destruction of stained glass and other ornaments which had been general during the reign of Elizabeth I. We have a vivid description in a letter of Dr. Reeves, the Dean:

> ... Sir Arthur Hazelrigg ... being entered the place, where the remainder of the Church Plate was, he commanded his servants to break down the wainscot round about the room, which was quickly done, they having brought crows of iron for that purpose ... Sir Arthur's tongue was not enough to express his joy, it was operative at his heels, for dancing and skipping (pray mark what music that is to which it is lawful for a Puritan to dance) he cried out, 'There boys; hark, hark it rattles, it rattles ...'

and later

> the common soldiers break down the organ and dashing the pipes with their pole-axes said, 'Hark how the organs go!'

With the occupation of Chichester and Arundel, Parliament had gained complete control of the county, and Royalist sympathisers were unable to continue open resistance without help from outside. This came 12 months later, with a dramatic advance by the Royalist General Hopton, helped by an early frost which made the muddy ways easier for horses and men. Hopton entered the county at the north-west corner via Petersfield on 5 December 1643 and arrived before Arundel on 6 December, after capturing on the way the fortified mansions of Stansted and Cowdray from small Parliamentary garrisons. Three days later Arundel Castle surrendered and a garrison of a thousand, including a hundred cavalry, was installed by Hopton.

96 *Bodiam Castle, 'slighted' interior*

XI *Parham: the Elizabethan mansion built by Sir Thomas Palmer in typical Elizabethan E-shaped form. A magnificent 160-foot-long gallery is located above the Great Hall.*

XII *Glynde Place: an Elizabethan mansion built by William Morley around a courtyard using flint and Caen stone.*

XIII *Bayleaf Farmhouse is a fine 'Wealden' type farm house of the 15th century, rebuilt at the Weald and Downland Open Air Museum at Singleton. In this example (left) the wing at the service end is jettied at the end as well as at the front. The open hall (below) has been furnished to show how it may have appeared in about 1540.*

Meanwhile Colonel Morley of Glynde, the local Parliamentary leader, collected what forces he could and made an appeal for help to Waller who commanded the Parliamentary forces in the Hampshire-Surrey region. Waller, aided in his turn by the continuing frost, responded immediately and crossed into Sussex and Hampshire on 17 December. Recapturing Cowdray on his way, he reached Arundel on the 19th, with a force of 10,000 men. Then followed a siege which lasted until the morning of 6 January 1644, when the whole garrison, reduced partly through the failure of the water-supply, surrendered. To quote a contemporary news writer: 'I never saw so many weak and feeble creatures together in my life, for almost all the common soldiers were half starved, and many of them hardly able to set one foot before another.'

Both the castle and the town suffered heavily, and that is one of the reasons why so much of Arundel dates from the 17th and 18th centuries, while the castle itself was almost entirely reconstructed in the 19th century—all but the Norman keep and the 14th-century Barbican gate being rebuilt in 19th-century Gothic with little relationship to the earlier building.

Sussex on the whole, particularly the eastern part of the county, suffered less disruption of its day-to-day life than many of the other English counties. After the second siege of Arundel it remained firmly in the control of Parliament, and, although some families were reduced to beggary by heavy

97 *View of Arundel from the south east in 1642. This print was made a year before the castle siege during the Civil War when it became a ruin. The view today of the reconstructed castle in 19th-century Gothic style bears little resemblance to the 17th-century building illustrated in the print, though the central Norman keep was faithfully restored.*

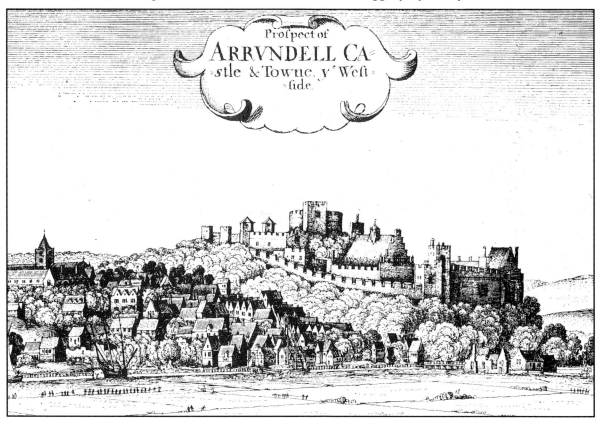

Profpect of ARRVNDELL CAstle & Towne, y West fide.

fines, the St Pancras suburb of Chichester destroyed, and a number of houses and castles in different parts of the county damaged and dismantled, life for most of the population returned to something like normality. As the conflict dragged on, however, there developed a growing resentment among farmers and villagers at the levies of food and the billeting of troops, a resentment not directed necessarily against either side but against the war itself. It was particularly strong in West Sussex where most of the earlier fighting had taken place. On 18 September 1645, a meeting of over a thousand villagers and farmers was organised at Rooks Hill (a name then generally used for the Trundle which still had on its crown a medieval chapel dedicated to St Roche). Other meetings were held at Duncton Down and Bury Hill. The local Parliamentary commanders took drastic action to suppress such protests since they regarded it as a movement of militant non-co-operation.

In spite of Parliament's control of Sussex, it was from the Sussex port of Shoreham that Prince Charles, escaping after the Battle of Worcester in 1651, secured a passage to France. Disguised as the servant of Colonel

98 *Civil War*

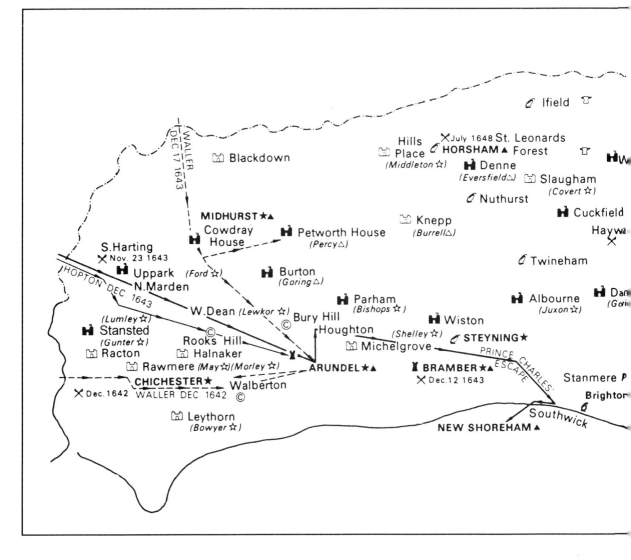

Gunter in Racton, whose horse he led, he managed to elude the Parliamentary controls at the two unavoidable river crossings at Houghton Bridge and Bramber.

It is not easy to assess the lasting effect of the Civil War in an area like Sussex. The material changes were relatively small and for many of the ordinary countryfolk the attitude of non-attachment to either side was probably fairly general—the political issues were not sufficiently clear-cut in terms that they could recognise. The majority in any case had no representation in Parliament as then constituted. The real effect was indirect and in the sphere of religion. A great many individuals had been forced to reconsider their attitude and crystalise their ideas. These individuals existed in every class and on both sides of the division. Just as there were many humble folk among the Sussex martyrs, who perished in the flames at Lewes and elsewhere at the time of the Reformation, so in the 17th century many of those who joined for conscience's sake one of the many sects such as the Baptists and the Quakers were drawn from the labouring and the smaller yeoman farmer class.

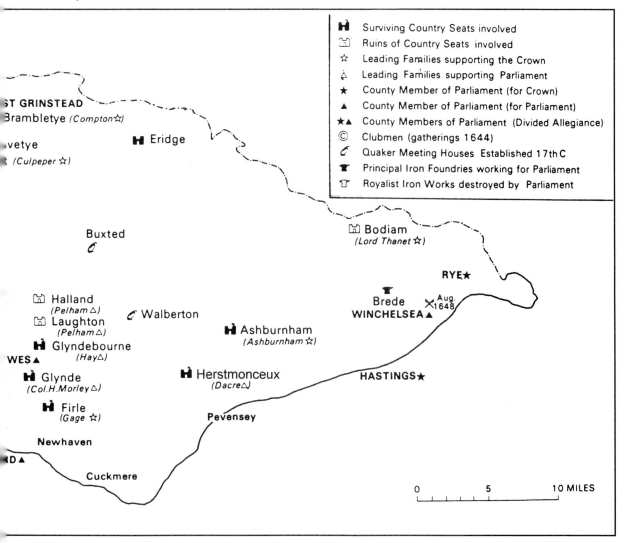

99 *Gunter family tomb, Racton, 1624*

George Fox, the founder of the Society of Friends, visited Sussex in 1655, and wrote in his Journal: 'I passed into Sussex and came to a Lodge near Horsham; where there was a great meeting and many were convinced.' Two years later he wrote: 'I travelled into Sussex visiting Friends, amongst whom I had great meetings; and many times I met with opposition from Baptists and other jangling professors, but the Lord's power went over them.' Before the end of the century more than a dozen regular Quaker Meetings had been established in different parts of the county. Two of the original Meeting Houses, the one at Coolham called the Blue Idol, and the one at Ifield, are still in use. Many of the early meetings were entirely rural congregations. William Penn is reported to have held Quaker Meetings at his house at Warminghurst, ten miles from a town of any size, attended by more than two hundred. In the Quarter Sessions Order Book at Chichester for 1684 is the following entry:

> William Penn being a factious and seditious person ... doth frequently entertain and keepe unlawfull assemblye and conventicle in his dwelling house at Warminghurst ... usually are assembled the number of one or two hundred unknown persons and sometimes more, to the terror of the King's liege people ...

During the early years they suffered a good deal of persecution including much of a petty kind such as the distraint of goods for the refusal to pay tithes out of all proportion to the amounts due, or the interruption of meetings with rotten eggs or stones. But there was also imprisonment and whipping, and between 1665 and 1690 nearly two hundred Quakers were imprisoned for varying periods in Horsham gaol.

The Baptists also were particularly strong in Sussex. In 1669 a survey was made of the Conventicles (or meetings) of the various nonconforming groups in the county. It is probably not complete, but it includes six Quaker congregations, the one at Steyning being estimated at two hundred; 11 Anabaptists, the largest congregation ('fifty to a hundred') being at Trotton; four Presbyterian groups, that at South Malling being estimated at 'at least five hundred'; and three gatherings of independents; there were also 24 others, not specifically named. There were, in addition of course, all those who remained loyal to the Catholic faith. These were particularly to be found among the great families. They had for long been used to practise their religion in secret; it was the period of priests' holes and concealed altars. At Slindon House, for instance, an elaborate series of three connected chambers were discovered during alterations in 1874; while at West Grinstead, in the 16th-century house adjacent to the new Catholic church, hidden in the roof there was a fully furnished chapel which has now been opened up and restored. With the easing of tension which culminated in the Toleration Act of 1689, secrecy was no longer necessary; it was then, for example, that the magnificent medieval chapel at Cowdray (which had presumably been carefully concealed during the seven-day visit of Queen Elizabeth in 1591) was restored and lavishly redecorated. But many Catholic families were financially ruined by the heavy fines imposed for recusancy; and they suffered particularly during the Commonwealth, when other nonconformist groups were on the whole left unmolested.

100 *'Blue Idol', Quaker Meeting House, Coolham*

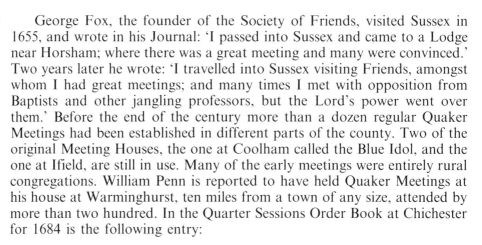

11

The 18th Century—Georgian Sussex

When the 18th century is considered in terms of the changing landscape of this country two things are apparent—first, the tremendous zest with which the landowners vied with one another in an endeavour to shape the landscape according to preconceived ideas of natural beauty: second, the revolution in agricultural methods and techniques which changed the shape of farms, fields and villages in many parts of England. Sussex had its full share of the first, though less of the second.

With the decline of the iron industry nature slowly reconstituted much of the oak forest and mixed woodland of the Weald. Towards the close of the 17th century this was helped forward by careful planting. As early as 1664, John Evelyn of Wootton (near the Sussex border in Surrey) advocated in *Sylva* a policy of systematic reafforestation: in fact, quick growing soft woods were often chosen to replace the indigenous woods. At the close of the 17th century landscaping was limited to the immediate environs of the great houses—artificial mounds, long terraces, avenues and orchards. All this was merely an extension of the Tudor walled and formal gardens which separated the house from wild and uncontrolled nature. Stimulated by the park at Versailles, and its English reflection in the avenues and canals added to the royal palace at Hampton Court, this developed into an obsession with grandeur and size—with the planting of broader, and taller, and ever longer avenues, which cut across hill and dale, in many cases for several miles. Few of these now remain in Sussex; the best example is perhaps the latest, the avenue at Stansted (1781), now crossed by the main road from Rowland's Castle to Emsworth, but still extending for two miles and providing a vista reaching to the Solent. These great avenues and vistas traversed the landscape but did nothing to mould it. The real triumph of the later 18th century was the development of landscaping on principles which followed, but at the same time organised and controlled, nature; and did both on the grand scale. Much of the Sussex landscape, not merely the remaining 18th-century parks, owes its quality to this considered control, whether in the planting of trees, such as the clump on Chanctonbury or round Singleton, the many lakes, apparently natural but in fact artificial, or the siting of 18th-century farms and cottages. The straight line, the dominant element in Renaissance garden planning, was succeeded by the curve, the casual, and the asymmetrical. 'Nature', wrote Capability Brown, the greatest of the 18th-century landscape gardeners, 'abhors a straight line.'

101 *Stansted Park and gardens, 1708*

A most interesting example of this change of approach can be seen by comparing the plan drawn up for the improvement of the park at Petworth House, some time early in the 18th century, with the park as laid out by Brown later in the century. The main features of the first are the great avenue stretching from the central façade for more than a mile to the west, the conversion of the rounded hill to the north into a series of terraces arranged like giant steps on the east, south and west sides and meeting at right-angles, and finally, beyond the hill to the north-west, a series of exactly similar rectangular fishponds divided by paths—a succession of straight lines reinforcing and reflecting the long lines of the house itself. The park was in fact later laid out with carefully placed but apparently natural clumps of trees, a lake with meandering curves and seemingly natural islands, and an open, turf covered hillside crowned with trees—not a straight line to be seen. The change in the material environment reflects a change in social attitudes. The pleasant informality at Petworth at the beginning of the last century contrasts with the rigid and somewhat humourless formality of Cowdray two centuries earlier.

> I really never saw such a character as Lord Egremont. 'Live and let live' seems to be his motto ... The very flies at Petworth seem to know there is room for their existence, that the windows are theirs. Dogs, horses, cows, deer and pigs, peasantry and servants, guests and family, children and parents, all share alike his bounty and opulence and luxuries. At breakfast, after the guests have all breakfasted, in walks Lord Egremont; first comes a grandchild, whom he sends away happy. Outside the window moan a dozen black spaniels, who are let in, and to them he distributes cakes and comfits, giving all equal shares. After chatting with one guest, and proposing some scheme of pleasure to others, his leathern gaiters are buttoned on and away he walks, leaving everybody to take care of themselves, with all that opulence and generosity can place at their disposal, entirely within their reach. Everything is solid, liberal, rich and English.

So wrote Benjamin Robert Haydon, in his diary, one of the many artists who were given hospitality.

Although all the great parks in Sussex, such as Cowdray, Arundel, **102** *Petworth Park* Petworth, Goodwood, Sheffield, Herstmonceux (to mention some which

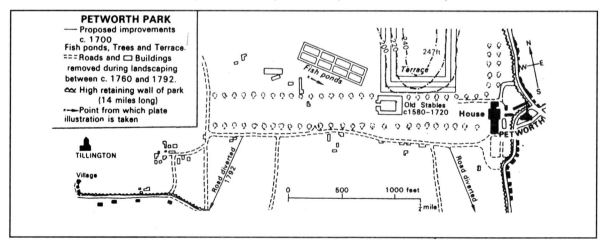

are open to the public), were reshaped in the 18th century under the influence of Capability Brown, in fact only four in the whole county were designed by him personally—Hills Place, near Horsham, Petworth, Ashburnham and Sheffield. Hills Place and Park were destroyed to make way for agriculture early in the 19th century, while both Ashburnham and Sheffield have been considerably altered. Sheffield Park in June and early autumn provides, round its lakes and connecting bridges (designed by Brown), a magnificent sequence of exotic flowering trees and shrubs with rich colouring, but these are all plantings of the Victorian period or later, and have little relationship to Brown's conceptions, which were based on the modification rather than the remaking of existing features, and he almost invariably used trees and shrubs native to the locality. The peculiarly English quality of the best 18th-century landscaping was often destroyed by the search for the exotic and the unusual in the 19th.

    This can be seen in one characteristic aspect of the period—the building of 'follies'. There is a world of difference between the elegance and practical usefulness of summer houses such as Carne's Seat in Goodwood Park or the now ruined Nore Hill folly in Slindon Park and the quite useless and visually inappropriate structures such as the Sugar Loaf at Brightling built at the beginning of the 19th century by the local landowner Jack Fuller to simulate the spire of a non-existent church, or the narrow chimney-like tower on Toat Hill above Pulborough. Somewhere between these two worlds of rational sophisticated leisure and romantic make-believe are the ruined summer house towers in Racton Park and Up Park, dating from the last quarter of the 18th century.

    Although some of the leading figures in the agricultural developments of the 18th century were Sussex farmers and landowners, the Sussex landscape

103 Petworth Park and House from the west. This view should be compared with the plan on page 102. The lake in the foreground covers the series of rectangular fish ponds and forms part of the landscaping carried out by Lancelot 'Capability' Brown during the mid-18th century. The house was built during the late 17th century but incorporates part of the 13th-century chapel of an earlier house.

did not suffer the dramatic change by enclosure which transformed the Midlands during this period. In Sussex enclosure had already taken place gradually and continuously from the time of the Black Death. What Sussex did share with other counties, particularly East Anglia, was an intense interest in new techniques of land improvement which created an agricultural revolution without which the expanding towns of the North could not have been fed and the industrial revolution would have been frustrated. The leadership came from the greater landowners, and in some cases from the larger yeoman farmers. The latter had increased in number steadily since Tudor and Stuart times at the expense of the smaller yeoman farmers, who had formed the core of the rural population in the 17th century and were the descendants of manorial tenants who had enclosed their holdings. These, with an equivalent number of poor cottagers, and landless agricultural labourers depending on wages, had formed the great bulk of the population; but by the mid-18th century this class had shrunk considerably. Some had sunk into the growing class of landless labourers, while a smaller number by skill and energy had become large-scale farmers. The Ellmans of Glynde are an excellent example of the latter. They had concentrated particularly on the improvement of the Southdown breed of sheep, both in weight and in quality of fleece. By the end of the 18th century they had become famous and the Southdown breed was known throughout the country. John Ellman, who died in 1832, still preserved an earlier tradition, housing his unmarried workers under his own roof, dining with them at a common table, and providing them with cottage and stock on marriage– a 19th-century version of the patriarchal quality of the medieval manor, but with a totally different and more flexible economic basis.

Perhaps the best example in Sussex of the great landowner devoting himself wholeheartedly to the scientific development of agriculture is that of the third Lord Egremont. The landowners by the possession of capital assets could promote large-scale schemes which were quite beyond the means of the wealthiest practising farmers. Lord Egremont financed the Rother navigation, the canal connecting Midhurst and Petworth with the Arun, in the hope of improving agriculture in the Rother area. Arthur Young in 1813 wrote: 'By this most useful and spirited undertaking, many thousand acres of land are necessarily rendered more valuable to the proprietors. Timber is now sent by water. Large falls [fellings] have been exported which would scarcely have been felled ... an additional tract of country is also supplied with lime from the Houghton and Bury pits ...'.

The general prosperity of agriculture in Sussex during the 18th century is reflected in the number of elegant houses built in towns and villages, and of farmhouses and labourers' cottages in the surrounding countryside. These almost always display that simplicity combined with good taste which was characteristic of the period. They reveal a feeling for the right use of materials—whether brick, stone or flint—and a sense of balance and proportion in the design of window and door space, or in the placing of decorative details. There is hardly a village without one or two good examples, while towns such as Lewes, Chichester and Arundel are probably

104 *Toat Tower, Pulborough, built 1827*

richer than any other towns of similar size in Britain. In the towns, owners were often content to rebuild the façade only; behind these façades may be found, on examination, buildings which may date from any period from the 14th century onwards.

Apart from these many new comfortable houses, the most striking general change that would have struck any traveller in Sussex towards the close of the 18th century, if he could have remembered the early or even the middle years, would have been the general increase in the amount of ploughland, the size of many of the fields, the large areas now growing root crops, and the almost complete disappearance of fallow, made possible by more scientific crop rotation.

Climax and Decline of Local Building Traditions

During the 17th and 18th centuries changes in building altered the appearance of every town and village—by the end of the 18th century these had transformed village and farmstead as to render them hardly recognisable to a visitor from the 15th.

105 *Racton Tower, built 1772*

The period from approximately the middle of the 16th to the middle of the 17th century has been described as that of 'the great rebuilding'. Almost every aspect of the townscape was altered; nor did the farmstead and cottage escape. It is not merely that almost all existing medieval houses were modified—occasionally so much so as to become unrecognisable—with added chimneys, altered windows, inserted floors and partitions, outshots and other extensions, but many more were pulled down and rebuilt in the new style. The new buildings often incorporated materials such as rafters and the main timbers from the buildings they replaced. Sussex, as much as any other county in the south-east, participated in this general revolution. The growth of population over the country as a whole seems to have been in the neighbourhood of fifty per cent, and in Sussex the increase is probably not much below the general level. This meant a tremendous amount of entirely new building, not only the extension of existing towns and villages, but also the building of new farmhouses and cottages away from the village on the now enclosed common fields.

This increase in building coincided with the developments in the use of brick. In combination with stone such as flint or the upper greensand, it greatly increased the possible uses of local stone. Since Sussex has a remarkably varied geological structure, with many different kinds of stone and clay, greater variety was given traditional building during this period than perhaps in any other English county. But these variations remained closely tied into, and sympathetic to, the landscape. The transport of heavy materials was no easier in the 17th or 18th centuries than it had been in the 13th, and in many areas of the Weald was probably more difficult. Once, therefore, timber was no longer the principal structural material, the geological pattern in Sussex conditioned much more completely the local pattern of building.

These geological divisions run from east to west so that the belts are still well defined by the visual character of the villages and farms along their

106 *Regency cottage,*
Brighton

length. Flint occupies the widest of these belts since it not only includes the whole of the Downland, but the coastal fringe from Selsey to Eastbourne. Along this coastal belt, but rarely extending above a couple of miles into the interior, rounded beach flint, or cobbles, were very generally used for every type of building. It is in the back streets of such towns as Brighton, Shoreham, or Worthing that much of the best remaining work of this kind can be seen.

From Worthing to Eastbourne, where the Downs and the sea meet, so that both the rough nodular flint from the former and the rounded cobble flint from the shore were equally available, many variations in the decorative exploitation of flint-graded selection, coursing, knapping and combination with other contrasting materials such as limestone or brick were developed. Many buildings in Chichester, Worthing and Brighton up to the second quarter of the 19th century were of flint. During the Regency period and after, many façades were covered with stucco, some with tile hanging, and still more recently by colour wash. Many inland villages escaped major transformations of this kind, such as Stanmer near Brighton, Slindon north of Arundel, or Singleton, north of Chichester. Variations also developed in the way brick and flint were combined. In the village of Slindon, for example, the use of brick to divide the flint work vertically is quite different from the more general practice of horizontal string courses.

In the area roughly bounded by Slindon on the west and Worthing on the east, there appeared during the last quarter of the 18th century highly elaborate uses of knapped flint. This was often combined with 'galletting', or the filling of the mortar joints with slivers of flint which accumulated in the process of knapping. This seems to have originated, or at least to have been given impetus locally, during the rebuilding of Goodwood House. The lodge gates on the north edge of the park bear the date 1784, and already represent a perfection of this technique, the knapping being so perfect that no brick is used for quoins, door or window jambs or lintels. All are built of meticulously squared flints laid in courses of brick-like precision. Within the next half century this was repeated on the Slindon Estate to the east, and the West Dean Estate to the west, culminating in the flint work to be seen in additions to West Dean House in the 1860s, which actually has hollow mouldings of knapped flint around windows and doorways. As so often happened, the fashion set by the great estates was copied by other builders in the area, and can be seen in buildings such as the Congregational Schools in Worthing, and in dozens of small houses and even cottages in this part of Sussex.

The great estates have played a large part in helping to maintain and develop local traditions, but their efforts have often been arbitrary, more concerned with the desire to assert their own individuality than to foster a genuine tradition. On the whole, in Sussex, the influence of the great estates—particularly in the western region—has been almost entirely beneficial, and has contributed a great deal to the preservation of a relationship between buildings and landscape.

The almost total dependence of the character of building on geological structure can perhaps best be seen in the long line of villages which stretch

107 *Pallant House, Chichester, now an historic house and art gallery. The house was built in 1712 by Henry 'Lisbon' Peckham, a wine merchant. Chichester contains some splendid examples of 18th-century domestic and public architecture particularly in the Pallants and St Martin's Square. The Pallants are found in the south-east quadrant of the city and reflect in miniature the city's main street plan.*

108 *South Street, Worthing, c.1825. Today, the houses on the left and in the centre have been transformed by inserted shop fronts, raised roofs, and surface stucco.*

109 *The Royal Crescent built in 1806 was Brighton's first residential terrace. After 1815, for a decade, expansion was particularly rapid and grandiose schemes such as that for Kemp town in 1825 on the East Cliff, and that for Brunswick town in Hove were started; both were only half completed, when the tide of popularity turned away from Brighton.*

110 *Bury church and village photographed at the turn of the century; a ferry is about to set off across the River Arun. The village lies on the upper greensand belt and almost all the buildings, including the church, are built with a greyish limestone or with brown sandstone from the lower green sandstone quarries above Pulborough.*

from east to west along the upper greensand belt just below the escarpment of the Downs. This stone is a very coarse limestone, and for this reason was only used, in preference to the flint obtainable immediately to the south, or the sandstone of the Hythe beds immediately to the north, when it could literally be quarried on the site. It is therefore a very narrow belt indeed in which this stone is employed, rarely more than a mile across; yet it gives quite a distinct homogeneous character to the villages situated along this outcrop.

The stone from the Hythe beds, which run in an outcrop parallel to the upper greensand some two or three miles to the north, was rather more widely used. It is a hard, warmly coloured sandstone both more durable, and more readily shaped, but even this stone is rarely seen more than a few miles from where it could be quarried. Villages such as Easebourne near Midhurst, or Upperton near Petworth, were built or rather rebuilt, in the 17th and 18th centuries almost entirely of stone quarried on the spot. This

stone was often named after a principal local quarry, hence Pulborough stone, or Easebourne stone.

The Weald clay was the source of three very different types of stone. One, often referred to as 'winklestone', or by various local names such as 'Kirdford marble', consists of consolidated snail shells; when cut and polished it presents a dark brown finely mottled surface not unlike Purbeck marble. The second is hard sandstone, often called 'ripplestone' from the ripple-marks formed on the sandbanks and beaches of the then inland sea preserved by an extraordinary coincidence of flooding and petrifaction over a hundred million years ago. Neither of these appreciably affect the exterior appearance of buildings, seldom being used for wall structure—winklestone was mainly used on internal decorative features, such as fireplaces, and ripplestone for floor paving. The third is the hard laminated sandstone used in the western Weald in every sort of building, from church to cottage, during the 17th and 18th centuries. As in the medieval period it was mainly used for roof covering, and this created something of a recognisably local style, since the weight of these tiles necessitated a lower pitch to the roof, and roof pitch is a very dominant feature in buildings. In the last hundred years a large proportion of these roofs have been replaced with lighter materials to reduce the weight on overburdened rafters, often with imported Welsh slate.

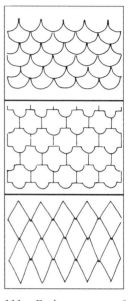

111 *Early patterns of hanging tiles.*

Within the area of the Central Weald, stretching from Crawley to Hastings, there are a number of seams of extremely fine sandstone. These do not dominate the local environment to quite the same extent as the more clearly defined areas of the flint and greensand belts, but there are very few villages in the area without a sprinkling of houses built in the 18th or early part of the 19th centuries from these fine local sandstones.

Brick itself was also given local qualities in its use. The clays in Sussex vary enormously and almost every parish contained a brickyard by the middle of the 18th century where bricks were made, often as a part-time or seasonal occupation, to meet the needs of the immediate area as they arose. The resulting variations in colour and technique often gave a distinctive quality to the buildings in the locality. In addition there were differences of colour, due to differences of heat in firing: just as the Tudor bricklayers had used colour variation to create diaper decorations, the even more striking contrasts, produced in the 18th-century kilns, between the deep red of the sides and the dark blue ends of the bricks suggested other forms of decoration; string courses and other structural lines could be picked out and emphasised by this method with recognisably regional forms. For example, the use of the blue ends or 'headers' to create large panels of blue within a framing of red 'stretchers' is a feature of both Midhurst in the west and of Lewes in the east of the county, but each in different ways.

In the latter half of the 17th century other materials were introduced in the northern parts of the county, the most notable being the development of tile-hanging as a means of wall-cladding. This became elaborated in the 18th century by the use of ornamental tiles of various patterns, differing also in colour according to the clay used. These were used to create many varieties of pattern, and some villages in the north west parts of the county,

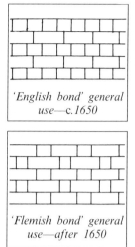

'English bond' general use—c.1650

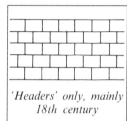

'Flemish bond' general use—after 1650

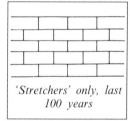

'Headers' only, mainly 18th century

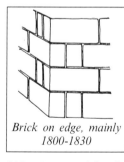

'Stretchers' only, last 100 years

Brick on edge, mainly 1800-1830

112 *Forms of brickwork*

where most of these ornamental tiles were produced, have been given a quite distinctive character as a result. Here we can see the way local traditions develop—the relationship of houses within a particular area to locally produced material. The process, however, was interrupted by the introduction of cheap and easy transport, before it reached the status of a genuine local style.

In the 18th century a particular kind of tile hanging which imitated brickwork and came to be known as 'mathematical tiling' was invented. Examples of this exist in almost every town in Sussex, such as the summer house in which Henry James the novelist worked for many years at his home at Rye. Unfortunately it was destroyed by a flying bomb. In the Brighton area a particularly striking form was the use of tiles with a deep purple glaze. One of the larger schemes was the Royal Crescent at Kemp Town, built in 1806, where the façade is covered entirely with such tiles over a flint rubble wall.

Parallel with the use of tile hanging in the northern and central parts of the county was the use of painted weatherboard in the eastern area. This was associated with the growing importation of sawn timber from the Continent particularly from the channel ports, one of which—Deal—gave its name to the type of soft pine woods unloaded there. Painted weatherboard houses of three storeys, built in the 18th century, are still in a good state of preservation although framed with pine instead of wealden oak. In other parts of the county it is found sporadically and is probably associated with the introduction of water powered saw mills, as at Blackstone village near Henfield, combined with an increasing supply of locally grown soft wood following the extensive replanting of areas devastated in the period of iron working.

In the 19th century there were a number of variations in the regional production and use of brick which might have become the basis for recognisably local styles, such as the use of bricks on edge for a couple of decades at the beginning of the century in a very high proportion of new buildings within a clearly defined area of the western Weald; or again, towards the close of the century, the use of yellow brick as a patterning element in the north-west corner of the county.

The period when the traveller through Sussex would have been most impressed by the variety of the local scene and, at the same time, the strongest sense of locality and the individual character of village and town, was in the half century between 1750 and 1800. By then most of the more attractive regional variations had been developed, the older traditions not yet wholly submerged, and the ultimate dependence in each area on the overall geological pattern still dominant. Local forms were still being evolved, only to be diluted and then lost with the coming of the canals and the railways.

12

Regency Sussex

By strict reckoning the Regency period is only the decade from 1811 when George III became finally and incurably insane, to 1820 when the Prince Regent ascended the throne as George IV, but it is usually used, as here, to cover roughly the period of the Napoleonic wars and the reign of George IV—approximately the thirty years from 1795 to 1825. It was during this period that the Pavilion, the Regency terraces, the squares and crescents of Brighton and Hove were built, and when large-scale schemes of development, not only in Brighton, but in Worthing and Bognor, were formulated, and partly completed.

Brighton was recorded in Domesday Book as a fishing village. It possessed a harbour of some importance, presumably where the Steine and Pool Valley are today, and flourished during the Middle Ages. It was fortified during the Hundred Years' War, and, at the time of the Armada still possessed a 'bulwark' which was renovated only to fall later under the assaults of the sea. Brighton's decline was, in fact, due partly to the silting of the harbour (as at Hastings) and partly to the sea's encroachments. Defoe, in his tour through England and Wales (1724), describes it as:

> A poor fishing town, old built and on the very edge of the sea ... the sea is very unkind to this town and has, by its continual encroachments, so gained upon them (the townspeople) that in a little time more they might reasonably expect it would eat up the whole town, above a hundred houses having been devoured by the water in a few years past, they are now obliged to get a brief granted them, to beg money all over England to raise banks against the water; the expenses of which will be eight thousand pounds which ... would seem to be more than all the houses in it are worth.'

Such was the town which Dr Russell of Lewes managed to popularise as a salt-water spa between 1750 and 1780. He advocated sea bathing and sea drinking as a cure for most ills and established a hydro where the *Albion Hotel* now stands. In 1783 the Prince of Wales first visited the town, returning again over the next two years to be with his morganatic wife, Mrs. Maria Fitzherbert. In 1786 he purchased a farmhouse, his 'Marine Pavilion', overlooking the Steine promenade. The following year the Pavilion was built to a design of Henry Holland in the record time of five months. It was then a simple Georgian villa. Between 1815 and 1822 further work was undertaken by the architect John Nash, who transformed Holland's building into the extravagance of oriental and eastern architecture we know today. The Prince lavished over half a million pounds on the project. Brighton continued to be his favourite residence until 1826. This set the seal on the place's growing popularity as a fashionable resort. In 1780 the population had been 3,600, already a sizable town for the period. By 1794 it had risen to 5,669; by 1801, to 7,337; and by 1821 to 21,429. It was in fact an increase which rivalled the most remarkable parallel developments in Lancashire and Yorkshire, but for entirely different reasons; and so it has continued ever since—for recreation, retirement and commuting from London. The first residential terrace—the Royal Crescent—was built in 1798 and the first decade of the 19th century. The Royal Stables and Riding School (now the Corn Exchange and the Dome) were designed by William Porden and built in 1804. With the death of George IV Brighton ceased to be the favourite resort of the monarchy. Much of the furniture of the Pavilion was removed to Buckingham Palace, and finally the shell of the building which had cost in all over half a million pounds was bought, as the result of a small majority vote, by the citizens of Brighton in 1850 for £50,000. Brighton has had no reason to regret this purchase: today, refurnished with much of the original furniture, it forms a major attraction.

During most of this period from 1796 to 1815 England was at war with France under Napoleon, and, for at least two years, from 1800 to 1802, a threat of invasion hung continuously over the South Coast. Troops were stationed behind Brighton, and guns had been set up at various points, many on the exact sites used over two hundred years before as gun emplacements against the expected Spanish Armada. Along all the flatter coast from Eastbourne to Kent, where the invasion fleet was expected to land, Martello towers were built; a considerable number of these remain, partly ruined or converted to various uses, such as the Wish Tower on the front at Eastbourne.

In the 10 years after 1815 expansion was particularly rapid and grandiose schemes such as that for Kemp Town in 1825 on the East Cliff, and for Brunswick Town in Hove were started; both were only half completed, when the tide of popularity turned away from Brighton. By the time it flowed again, after the opening of the Brighton to London railway in 1841, fashion had changed, and the ordered and dignified terraces, squares and communal gardens of the Regency development gave place to the individualism and petty pretentiousness of the Victorian era.

What happened at Brighton was followed, though on a smaller scale, very closely in Worthing and, through the enterprise of Sir Richard Hotham, in Bognor. Hotham a wealthy London hatter, began to develop Bognor, or Hothampton, in 1787. The name of his new 'garden town', which he aimed to establish as a select resort, never materialised. Hotham hoped that the Royal family would visit his resort and Dome House was built for their use. Princess Charlotte, George III's daughter, was the only one to patronise the town: there was one visit from the Prince of Wales. Worthing owes its development at the turn of the 19th century to its patronage by Princess Amelia who visited in 1798. The town was built around the former fishing village. Eastbourne, by contrast, despite being patronised by George III's children in 1780, staying at Sea Houses, had to wait until the mid-19th century before being developed into a popular resort by William Cavendish, the seventh Duke of Devonshire, and John Dawes Gilbert.

113 *French invasion fantasy, 1804*

In 1801 the population of Worthing was approximately 1,000; in 1831, approximately 5,000; that of Bognor in 1801, about 700, and in 1831, nearly 3,000.

It is in this period that the turnpike system and the stage coach reached the peak of their development. Cobbett wrote in 1823: 'Brighton is so situated that a coach, which leaves at not very early in the morning, reaches London by noon: and starting to go back in two hours and a half afterwards reaches Brighton not very late at night. Great parcels of stock-jobbers stay at Brighton with the women and children. They skip backward and forward on the coaches and actually carry on stockjobbing in Change Alley though they reside in Brighton.' This perfection of the London to Brighton coaching system led to Brighton becoming for a few years the main cross-channel port of England. Before the development of the railway, there was little difference between the speed of the early cross-channel steam-packets and the stage coach, and Brighton, not Dover or the ports to the east, lay on the direct route from London to Paris. A chain pier, destroyed in a storm in 1896, was built in 1823 to enable passengers to embark directly onto the packet boats from the coaches, without the intermediary of unstable rowing boats and the broad shoulders of the ferry-men. A few years later, the building of the railway in 1847 and the improvement of Newhaven harbour brought this to an end; soon afterwards the Brighton Packet Boat fleet was sold to the railway company. Then, in its turn, Newhaven declined in competition with Folkestone and Dover, for railway speeds became so much faster that the longer land routes with shorter channel crossing became more attractive.

Inland the new canals, turnpikes and the continuing expansion of agriculture, were gradually changing the face of the countryside. The Regency period made itself felt by the widespread imitation in town and village of the stucco used in the fashionable terraces of Brighton and Hove. Innumerable brick, flint, stone and even timber cottages and houses were indiscriminately plastered over and painted. The creeping rot of urban-inspired uniformity had begun.

Smuggling

Attempts to smuggle goods are inevitable whenever the State, or independent authorities, levy tolls or taxes on the free passage of goods. The greater the tax the greater the incentive, and the larger the number of goods affected the more widespread the traffic becomes. Smuggling, or the evasion of toll and tax, has been rife in Sussex since Saxon times. In the 13th century there was continual conflict, for instance, between the merchants of Shoreham and William de Braose concerning the right and extent to which, as lord of the manor, he could levy tolls. De Braose, for example, claimed from each ship calling there with wine 'one cask from before the mast and one cask from behind the mast', but the merchants denied the claim to the second cask. Lives were endangered in at least one affray between agents of de Braose and the townsmen. Smuggling on an organised scale began when the Crown first imposed an embargo or a tax on a main article of export—wool-fells. This particularly affected Sussex, which was one of the chief

114   *Contraband*

areas of wool production, and in the 13th century wool was a principal export. To control the trade, Wool Staples were established through which all wool destined for export was required to be registered on payment of the export duty. In Sussex the Staples were at Lewes and Chichester. And so the smuggling traffic began—a traffic eventually to be organised on an international scale.

For nearly three centuries wool remained the basis of smuggling in Sussex; although wool is singularly bulky, and the rewards relatively small, the traffic in wool continued right into the 18th century. Defoe, in his *Tour through England and Wales* in 1722, observed in the marsh lands round Rye and Winchelsea:

> Dragoons riding about as if they were huntsmen beating up their game ... in quest of owlers, as they call them ... often times they are attacked in the night ... and sometimes killed ... and obliged as it were to stand still and see the wool carried off before their faces, not daring to meddle, the boats taking it from the very horses' backs ... are on the coast of France before any notice can be given of them.

About the time of the first interference with the free export of wool, an embargo was placed on the import of base coin from the Continent. The Statute of Treason in 1351 made this a capital offence, but, as in the case of wool, enforcement proved almost impossible. It is not unreasonable to suppose that those who smuggled wool out from the Sussex coast safely brought back forbidden coinage, so much easier to handle and dispose of, on their return. Gradually a permanent underground organisation grew up with very wide contacts; thus it was simple to transfer attention to other commodities whenever restrictions were imposed. In the 16th century, when the export of cannon without licence was forbidden, there was widespread smuggling of cannon, certainly the most difficult commodity ever to be tackled. In this unlawful traffic many of the great landowners, with their interests in the new iron-works, became involved. The brothers Sir Anthony and Sir Robert Shirley of Wiston combined their activities as official ambassadors or agents of the Crown in different parts of Europe and the Mediterranean with the unofficial sale of armaments from the various iron-works in which they had shares. Sir Anthony even managed to place orders with the Shah of Persia.

In the 17th century, during the Civil War, bullion and armaments were smuggled from the Continent on behalf of Charles I. A hundred and fifty years later, during the Napoleonic War, political *emigrés*, or escaped English soldiers were smuggled over from France, while bullion and documents, or escaped French prisoners of war were shipped as contraband from England with complete political impartiality.

Undoubtedly the golden age of smuggling in Sussex was the 18th century. It then achieved the position of a major industry, when squire and parson, burgher and peasant, were all involved. During this century the levying of customs and excise duties became a principal element in government finance; national solvency, in fact, in the days before income tax, depended on the increase of indirect taxation. The number of dutiable or restricted articles increased from a dozen or so to several hundred (for a brief period even salt was taxed). Most of these goods were far easier to handle, or conceal, than wool had been. Small barrels of spirits could be dropped overboard, to lie concealed in muddy estuaries: seven pounds of tea, taxed at 20s. on the pound, produced a reward quite out of proportion to the older traffic in wool. Since articles such as these were consumed by every section of the population, there was general sympathy with the professional smuggling fraternity. A good deal of casual labour was recruited from the agricultural population. A man could earn 'on the side' one pound a day (considerably more than the equivalent of a week's wages on the land) as a 'runner', carrying the goods from the coast to the secret depots in the vicinity of London.

This highly-organised industry, in which hundreds of men were involved professionally, was opposed by preventive measures which were inefficient and inadequate; this often led to an overweening confidence on the part of the smuggling gangs. In 1747 a notorious Sussex group known as the Hawkhurst gang laid siege to, and broke open, the Customs House at Poole, where goods, seized by preventive officers, had been stored. The fear and hatred of spies and informers also led to drastic measures against anyone suspected of laying information. The particularly brutal murder of two supposed informers, Chater and Galley, a short time after this led to the capture and trial of several of this particular gang. Seven were condemned to death at the assizes held at Chichester in 1749, two being hanged in chains on Selsey Bill, another on the Trundle, and another on the highway at Rake, as a warning to others. The savagery of the law itself often led desperate men, whose lives were already jeopardised through having been involved in some affray, to further acts of desperation. As late as 1810 a gang of this type, known as the Copthorne gang, terrorised the area east of Crawley.

Since the middle of the 16th century assizes had been held almost always at either Horsham or East Grinstead. In 1775 a new gaol was built at Horsham to replace one built in 1640—'the foundations to be three feet deep of hard Horsham stone, the building itself of burnt stock bricks; all timber to be heart oak, tyled roof on heart oak laths'. It was in fact the first 'model' prison in England with separate cell accommodation for the new regime of solitary confinement for all prisoners convicted of felony. Only debtors continued to remain communally housed. The prison reformer John Howard visited the prison in 1782 and highly approved of it. 'This county', he wrote, 'has set the noble example of abolishing all fees and also "the tap" (the purchase of drink by prisoners). In consequence I found the gaol as quiet as a private house, the prison as clean, healthy and well regulated.' In 1843 a new county gaol was built at Lewes and after that Lewes became the sole assize town in Sussex.

In 1788 a subsidiary prison or 'House of Correction' was built at Petworth to supplement the county gaol at Horsham. This was designed by James Wyatt and for some years shared with the new gaol at Horsham the distinction of being the most up to date prison in the whole country, incorporating also the new system of solitary confinement. It also had an elaborate machine which recorded on a dial called an 'Ergometer' the exact amount of energy each prisoner put into turning a crank. For a time these two prisons served

115 *Treadmill, Horsham gaol*

as models for the efficiently planned but utterly inhuman institutions built in almost every county during the next half century. The 'House of Correction' at Petworth was pulled down in 1881, a small section—the governor's house—being incorporated in the present police headquarters.

The assize weeks at Horsham were highly popular events and regularly attracted thousands of visitors who poured in by waggon or on foot, and camped on the great common, north of the town. The last public hanging on the common was in 1820; but there were other public spectacles such as whipping at the cart's tail, standing in the pillory, or sitting in the stocks.

The severity or brutality of punishments however seem to deter less than the certainty of being caught; and the final suppression of smuggling depended on two things—the development of a really effective preventive system, and a lessening of the rewards to be gained by smuggling, by a progressive lowering of taxation on a great many of the highly-taxed commodities. Both these things happened in the years which followed the final defeat of Napoleon. The Navy, released from the task of fighting a major war, was able to turn its attention to the smugglers; and an extremely efficient Coastguard system was established—an appropriate employment for retired, or now redundant, naval personnel. Along the whole circuit of the English coast, there were set at intervals coastguard stations, each within signalling distance of the next, and each linked to its neighbour by a path which was patrolled every night. Beyond, swift cutters patrolled the sea itself. Within ten years, large-scale smuggling was ended, and though a trickle still continues even today, it is limited to a narrow range of small, but valuable, commodities such as drugs; it has little relationship to the large-scale mass organisation of its heyday when it is reckoned that perhaps as much as one third of the tea, spirits and tobacco consumed in this country had escaped duty.

Just as the decline of the ports in the 15th century, or of the iron industry in the 17th, led many honest burghers or iron-workers to turn to smuggling for a living, so in the 1830s unemployment and distress in Sussex was certainly increased by the successful suppression of smuggling. The following is a quotation from a report on the 'Disturbed Districts of Sussex', published in 1833. 'Since the establishment of the Preventive Service, smuggling is much diminished. This diminution has had the effect of increasing the Poor Rate ... those who do not directly profit by smuggling consider that it is advantageous as finding employment for many who otherwise would be thrown on their parishes.'

116   *Portable whipping post and stocks*

13

Cobbett's Sussex

Between 1822 and 1825 William Cobbett toured Sussex four times. His vivid account of these journeys is an excellent starting point from which to look at the rural life of the county during the first decades of the last century. Cobbett had been brought up as a farmer, and he saw the landscape with the eyes of a farmer; he judged the changes of the period by how they affected the men who worked on the land, and the kind of crop that the land sustained. He had little sympathy with the Regency developments at Brighton or with the Court: 'This place is a great resort with the "whiskered" gentry ... Whence came the means of building these new houses and keeping the inhabitants? Do they come out of trade and commerce? Oh no! They come from the land ... .' In contrast he says: 'The farm houses have been growing fewer and fewer, the labourers' houses fewer and fewer; and it is manifest to every man who has eyes to see with that the villages are regularly wasting away ... In all the really agricultural villages and parts of the kingdom, there is a shocking decay, a great dilapidation and constant pulling down ... .' Although Cobbett tended to exaggerate, we must remember that he was writing in a period of temporary agricultural depression. The high price of corn and the tremendous impetus given to agriculture during the Napoleonic War had led to the ploughing up of great areas previously uncultivated, as well as to general improvements through the use of new machinery and techniques. This boom prosperity had been followed, as after the war of 1914-18, by a rapid fall in agricultural prices, the bankruptcy of many small farmers, and the inability of even the better and more efficient ones to pay adequate wages.

117　*Toll booth, Falmer*

The situation varied a great deal between one part of the country and another; within the county of Sussex there was no uniformity. On his journey via Petworth and Duncton to Singleton and Funtington, Cobbett writes: 'There is, besides, no misery to be seen here. I have seen no wretchedness in Sussex; nothing to be at all compared to that which I have seen in other parts; and as to these villages in the South Downs, they are beautiful to behold ... I saw, and with great delight, a pig at almost every labourer's house. The houses are good and warm; and the gardens some of the very best that I have seen in England. ' Elsewhere he speaks of: 'The walks and the flower borders, and the honeysuckles and the roses framed over the doors and over arched sticks that you see in Hampshire, Sussex and Kent, that I have many a time sitten upon my horse to look at so long and so

118 *Toll House, Lind-field*

often, as greatly to retard me on my journey. Nor is this done for show or ostentation. If you find a cottage in these counties, by the side of a bye lane, or in the midst of a forest, you find the same care about the garden and the flowers.' Writing of Horsham (and he writes in a similar vein of Lewes and Billingshurst): 'This is a very nice, solid, country town. Very clean, as all the towns in Sussex are. The people very clean. The Sussex women are very nice in their dress and in their houses. The men and boys wear smock frocks more than they do in some counties. When country people do not they always look dirty and comfortless.'

Describing the wealden area between East Grinstead and Crawley he says: 'The labouring people look pretty well. They have pigs. They invariably do best in the woodland countries ...'. And again, when comparing the corn country of Thanet with that of Sussex: 'What a difference between the wife of a labouring man here and the wife of a labouring man in the forests and woodlands of Sussex! Invariably have I observed that the richer the soil, and the more destitute of woods, that is to say, the more purely a corn country, the more miserable the labourers.'

Cobbett mentions new enclosures in Sussex in a number of passages; such enclosures were confined almost entirely to the commons and wastes, and in many areas caused hardship and distress. On his ride from Worth to Horsham in 1822 he noted: 'This forest ... is followed by a large common, now enclosed, cut up, disfigured, spoiled, and the labourers all driven from its skirts. I have seldom travelled over eight miles so well calculated to fill the mind with painful reflections.' This refers to the great common which stretched to the north-east of Horsham and was enclosed by the lord of the manor, the eleventh Duke of Norfolk, by an Enclosure Act passed in 1813. Of the 800 acres involved, the bulk was acquired by the Duke, and the cost of the enclosure met by the sale of a small part. By 1911 land thus acquired was fetching £850 per acre. No doubt as a small compensation to the burgesses of Horsham, he rebuilt the Town Hall in a singularly ugly pseudo-Norman style.

On the whole, west Sussex seems to have been more prosperous than the eastern parts of the county. He speaks of the extensive emigration to America of pauperised agricultural labourers from the eastern areas of Sussex; it was in the eastern areas, only a few years later, that distress and unrest reached breaking point.

Cobbett, with the exception of his journey to Battle in January 1822, travelled invariably on horseback, and he has a good deal to say about the turnpike roads. As a farmer his appreciation was mixed with criticism. His attitude is very different from that of Defoe, just a hundred years earlier. Defoe described with enthusiasm the new system by which Turnpike Trusts were authorised to levy tolls on road users to meet the costs of re-making and maintaining the most important highways. Up to then the responsibility had been that of the local parishes. Defoe speaks of the first turnpike in Sussex, which dealt with the road from Godstone to East Grinstead into the central Weald: 'The great Sussex road, which was formerly insufferably bad, is now become admirably good.' But later he writes of the 'appalling conditions of other Sussex roads', in particular of Stane Street 'the old Roman road' which crossed 'a terrible deep country called the Homeward (Holmwood) and so to Petworth and Arundel; but we see nothing of it now; and the country indeed remains in the utmost distress for want of good roads.'

It was not until 1749 that the first entirely Sussex Turnpike Trust was set up 'for the repairing the road from Hindhead Heath through Fernhurst lane and Midhurst to the city of Chichester in the county of Sussex'. The preamble to the Act describes 'Many parts thereof so ruinous and deep in the winter season that carriages cannot pass without great danger and difficulty ...'. The Trustees, mostly local Justices of the Peace, were authorised to let the Tolls 'for any term not exceeding seven years, or to appoint collectors'. The Act also authorised the amount of tolls to be levied,

> For every coach, berlin, landau, chariot, chaise, calash, chair, caravan, or hearse, etc. drawn by six horses or mules, 1/-; if drawn by four, nine pence, if drawn by two, six pence, or by one horse, three pence. For every waggon, wain, cart ... if drawn by six horses or oxen one and six, if by four, nine pence, and so on for one horse, mule, etc., unladen, one penny for every drove of oxen, ten pence per score. Calves, sheep, etc., five pence ...

This Act represents the general form of the many Turnpike Acts for the county of Sussex which followed in rapid succession. These piecemeal improvements resulted in a rather haphazard system, both of finance and maintenance. Many of the Trusts covered very short lengths of road; only

119 *The Toll Cottage at Bramber, showing the gates and general arrangement of the turnpike road. A similar toll cottage, from Beeding, has been reconstructed at the Weald and Downland Open Air Museum.*

one exceeded 30 miles. In the report on the Turnpike Trusts of the County which was issued in 1857, 51 Trusts are enumerated, covering 640 miles of road with 238 toll gates or bars, an average of one gate to every two and a half miles. On the 23-mile turnpike from Mayfield to Wadhurst there were 19 gates. The longest section under a single Trust was that from Brighton to Cuckfield and West Grinstead, a matter of 35 miles with 16 gates. Ten of the Trusts covered sections of the road less than five miles in length. The concept of making the user pay was not unsound in theory, but in practice inefficient and costly to enforce. The delays at the gates, the maintenance of the 238 collectors, and the 238 toll cottages and barriers was uneconomic and the system of farming out the collection of tolls by leasing them, though eliminating the need for a great deal of supervision, led also to abuses of other kinds.

The toll cottages were mostly purpose-built, and, though amongst the tiniest cottages built at that time, were often well designed, using traditional local materials. Occasionally an existing building or part of a building—like the one in the centre of Lindfield—was used. Those which were purpose-built seem invariably to have followed a standard pattern of two rooms, usually separated by a central chimney, each measuring from ten to twelve feet square. Perhaps some forty still survive, but their number diminishes

120 *The Turnpike roads*

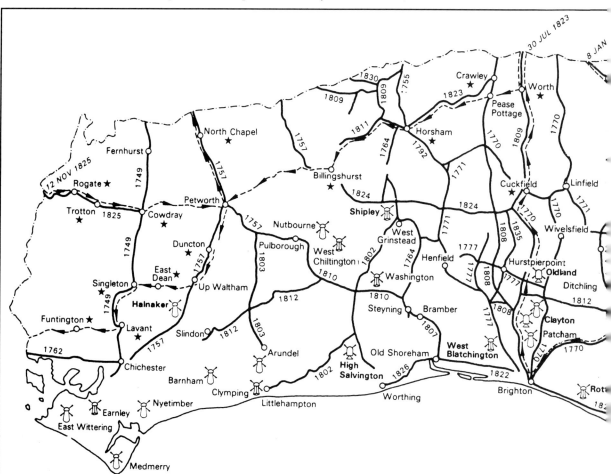

year by year, simply because of their excessively close proximity to the roads which still remain the network of the county today.

By Cobbett's time, the Sussex turnpike system was virtually complete, and the organisation of the coaching system on roads such as that from London to Brighton could hardly be carried further, whether in the quality and lightness of coach construction, the grading of inclines and road surfaces, or the perfect timing in the changing of horses at the posting stations. Cobbett admired the perfection achieved, but disliked the ends that it served. They benefited, as he saw it, mainly the wrong people. 'North Chapel is a little town in the Weald of Sussex where there were formerly post chaises, but where there are none kept now ... the guests at inns are now commercial gentlemen who go about in gigs instead of on horseback.' He resented the differential tolls on the size of wheels, which, as he saw it, penalised the farmer. 'This is the time thought proper to enact that the whole of the farmers in England should have new wheels to their waggons and carts, and that they shall be punished by the payment of heavier tolls.' On the Worthing turnpike, for instance, in 1824, the toll on any waggon, wain, dray or cart with wheels of less than 4½ inches was 3d., for waggons etc. with wheels of 4½-6 inches, 2d., and for waggons etc. with wheels of 6 inches or over, 1d.—a threefold difference. In other words, the farmers were encouraged to

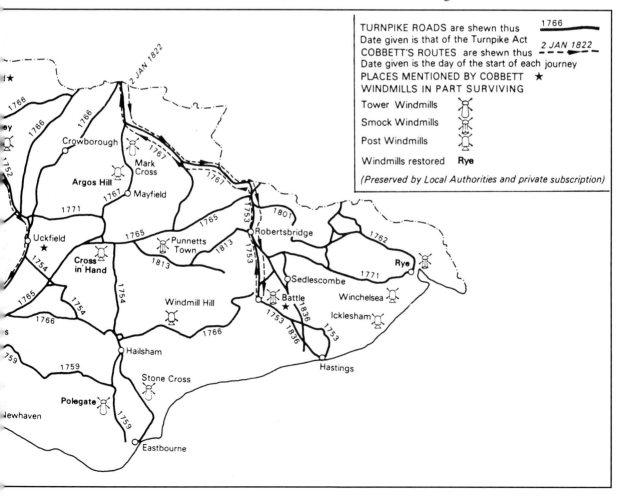

A TABLE of the TOLLS payable at this TURNPIKE GATE.
[By the Local Act.]
s d

FOR every Horse, Mule, Afs, or other Beast (Except Dogs) drawing any Coach, Berlin, Landau, Barouche, Chariot, Chaise, Chair, Hearse, Gig, Curricle, Whiskey, Taxed Cart, Waggon, Wain, Timber frame, Cart frame Dray or other Vehicle of whatsoever description when drawn by more than one Horse or other Beast the Sum of Four pence half penny Such Waggon, Wain, Cart, or other such Carriage having Wheels of lefs breadth than four and a half inches .... 4 1⁄2

AND when drawn by one Horse or other Beast only the sum of six pence (Waggons, Wains and other such Carriages having Wheels as aforesaid) ... 6

FOR every Dog drawing any Truck, Barrow or other Carriage for the space of One Hundred Yards or upwards upon any part of the said Roads, the Sum of One Penny 1

FOR every Horse, Mule, Afs, or other Beast laden or unladen and not drawing, the Sum of Two-pence 2

FOR every carriage moved or propelled by Steam or Machinery or by any other power than Animal power the Sum of one Shilling for each Wheel thereof .... 1·0

FOR every Score of Oxen, Cows or neat Cattle, the Sum of Ten-pence and so in Proportion for any greater or lefs Number 10

FOR every Score of Calves, Sheep, Lambs or Swine the Sum of Five pence and so in proportion for any greater or lefs Number 5
(By 4, G. 4, C.95)

FOR every Horse, Mule, Afs or other Beast drawing any Waggon Wain, Cart or other such Carriage having the Fellies of the Wheels of the breadth of Six Inches or upwards at the Bottom when drawn by more than one Horse, Mule, Afs or other Beast the Sum of Three-pence 3

AND when drawn by one Horse, Mule, Afs or other Beast the Sum of Four-Pence (Except Carts) 4

FOR every Horse, Mule, Afs or other Beast drawing any Waggon Wain, Cart or other such Carriage having the Fellies of the Wheels of the Breadth of four inches and a half and lefs than Six inches when drawn by more than one Horse, Mule, Afs or other Beast the Sum of Three-pence three farthings .... 3 3⁄4

AND when drawn by one Horse, Mule, Afs or other Beast the Sum of Five-pence (Except Carts) 5

FOR every Horse, Mule, Afs or other Beast drawing any Cart with Wheels of every Breadth when drawn by only one such Animal the Sum of Six Pence 6

NB Two Oxen or neat Cattle drawing shall be considered as one Horse
3, G. 4, C.126.

CARRIAGES with four Wheels affixed to any Waggon or Cart all as if drawn by two Horses, Carriages with two Wheels so d pay Toll as if drawn by one Horse but such Carriages are Tolls if conveying any Goods other than for Protection.

121 *Table of tolls from Northchapel.*

fit wider wheels to their slow and heavy farm waggons, which would then serve to roll out the ruts created by the swifter narrow-wheeled coaches. Cobbett, instead of regarding this as a concession to the broad-wheeled waggon, saw it as penalising the farmer for the benefit of the coaching traffic.

Cobbett also regrets the way in which roads which had not been turnpiked were scorned and neglected. On his journey from Petworth to Lavant he wished to avoid going round by the turnpike through Chichester. 'In cases like mine, you are pestered to death to find out the way to get from place to place. The people you have to deal with are innkeepers, ostlers and post boys; and they think you mad if you express your wish to avoid turnpike roads, and a great deal more than half mad if you talk of going even from necessity by any other road. They think you a strange fellow if you will not ride six miles on a turnpike road rather than two on any other road.' In other words, the canalising of traffic onto the main highways had already begun.

Yet this great system of turnpike roads, coaches and coaching inns, in which a vast amount of capital had been invested, began within twenty years to crumble in face of the new transport revolution of the railways. The last turnpike to be constructed in Sussex was in 1841 between Cripps Corner in the central Weald and Hawkhurst. That same year the Brighton to London railway was opened. By 1870 most of the Turnpike Trusts in Sussex had been wound up and hundreds of coachmen, coachbuilders and others put out of business.

The Changing Pattern of Farm and Farmstead

Until the Middle Ages there were only two periods when changes in the techniques of farming and farm management took place so rapidly that they can be described as revolutionary. Both were the result of conquest. The first was the introduction of large scale estate farming by the Romans;

the second was the introduction of collective farming by the Saxons towards the end of the fifth century. The Saxon system lasted over much of the county for almost a thousand years.

The changes which began to take place towards the end of the Middle Ages with the breakdown of this collective farming system started gradually. They affected not merely the organisation and lay-out of farms and farm buildings, but the whole way of life of the countryside, and it is a still continuing process. The first phase in this development was the consolidation of holdings and their management, the second the steady improvement in technology involving greater capital investment, thus placing a premium on the increase in the size of holdings. In the later Middle Ages these tendencies were to be seen in the large scale farming practised by some of the monastic establishments, particularly by the Cistercians whose barns astonish by their size, and their sheep farming by its scale. But with the possible exception of some of the estates managed by the Abbey of Battle, and the great Cluniac Priory of St Pancras at Lewes, there is not much evidence for estate farming of this kind in Sussex. There is, however, considerable evidence to suggest that some of the largest and richest farms of the later Middle Ages were to be found in the mixed farming areas of the Weald where individual holdings had slowly developed from assarts cleared, and brought into cultivation, by pioneer families. Here, judging from 14th- and 15th-century

122 Findon Fair. This annual event on Nepcote Green is the largest sheep fair in Sussex. It has medieval origins and was traditionally held on 14 September but the date was changed in the late 1950s to the second Saturday in September. The writer, Barclay Wills, can be seen in the foreground with a shepherd.

123 & 124   *The exterior and interior of the magnificent aisled tithe barn at Alciston. Originally belonging to Battle Abbey, part dates from the 15th century, and there were later extensions.*

125   *Granary, Eastergate*

returns of the woollen trade, sheep farming, as on the Downs, was closely integrated with arable, and land may have been kept in good heart, giving continuous crop production, by the systematic folding of sheep between harvest and sowing. Farming in these areas would also have been combined with the husbandry of timber, providing additional winter employment. This type of mixed economy was still characteristic of the Weald after its slow reafforestation and recovery following the industrial interlude of hammer forge and blast furnace.

Bearing in mind that the enclosure of the great open common fields in the rest of the county had been largely completed by the end of the 16th century, it is probable that over the county as a whole there was, by the 17th century, the largest number of independent farmers and smallholders that Sussex has ever contained.

The next step was a steady increase in the size of farms in those areas suited to the application of the improved farming techniques of the 18th and 19th centuries. These areas were particularly those stretching from the greensand belt through the Downs and over the coastal plain, rather than the more acid and heavier soils of the Weald. The wealden farmer was therefore, except in a few favourable areas, left behind, and it was possible for Arthur Young, writing at the close of the 18th century, to describe the Weald as a backward area of relatively small farms compared with the progressive farming by then to be found in the larger farms of the Downland and coastal plain. In his first report on the agriculture of Sussex he writes, 'A person viewing the Weald from these hills, would immediately be struck with some degree of surprise at the prodigious proportion of woodland as the country under view appears one uniform mass. This arises partly from the woods being extensive and in part from a most barbarous inveterate practice, when the country was cleared, of leaving a belt of wood several yards wide round every distinct field as a nursery of timber.' He had no reservations as to the desirability of the increase in large scale farming in the Downland and the coastal plain. 'No doubt exists in my own mind ... from the observation which I have made, of the comparative superiority of great over small farms from every point of view.' He contrasts the traditional farming of the Weald with the new large scale farms. 'In the Weald, although farms sometimes rise to £200, ... a far greater number fall very considerably below this ... the average size is under £100 a year. On the South Downs they rise much higher. Many farmers occupy the greatest part if not the whole of their respective parishes, as in Bottolph's, Kingston, Coombes, Bramber, North Stoke, Bletchington, Falmer, Piddinghoe, and many others in the neighbourhood of Lewes, Eastbourne and Brighton.' In other words, these villages, once the centre of a collectively organised agriculture, had become single units little differing perhaps from Roman estates farms of the second and third centuries. Yet the mechanisation of farming had in many ways only just begun. 'Thrashing the wheat is everywhere performed by flail-work and cleaned either with a shovel and broom or by winnowing machines. He mentions three instances of 'thrashing machines ... at Bognor, Ashburnham and Petworth ... the prodigious saving

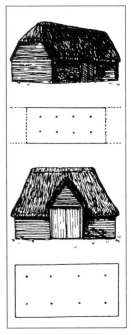

126 *Local types of aisled barns*

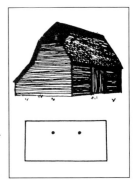

127 *Regional form of single aisled barn*

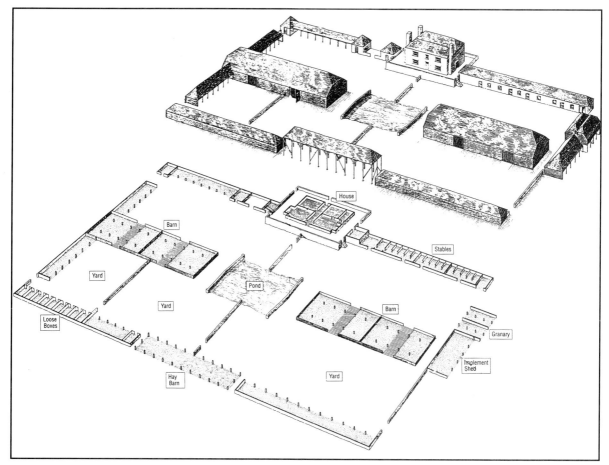

House

Barn

Stables

Yard

Pond

Yard

Loose
Boxes

Barn

Granary

Implement
Shed

Hay
Barn

Yard

128 *Stag Park, Pet-worth. The magnificent model farmstead built in 1782 by the third Earl of Egremont at the north-ern end of Petworth Park. The whole area was cleared, drained and prepared for cultivation.*

that might be made in the expenses of labour ... by substituting machinery ... ought to induce gentlemen and large farmers ... to improve this branch of rural economy.'

All these changes are reflected in the farms and farm buildings built before the present century. The most characteristic and universal of these is the barn, whether for storing grain before threshing, or hay for fodder. With very few exceptions the surviving medieval barns in Sussex are either the barns belonging to the Church, or manorial barns; few are associated with independent farmers, and these are almost all relatively small barns in the Wealden area. Large barns, such as the great aisled barn at Alciston, were mostly associated with the granges belonging to one of the greater monasteries—in the case of Alciston, Battle Abbey. It is not until the 16th and 17th centuries that we find large barns associated with the new yeoman farmer class. The majority of the greater barns found in the downland and coastal plain appear to have been built during the hundred and fifty years from the end of the 17th to the middle of the 19th centuries. They are quite clearly the result of the increase in corn yields, coupled with the increase in the size of farms.

It was during this period that various regional types of barn became established. A form which is widespread in the coastal plain is aisled on both sides and is seldom less than five bays, and very often of nine or ten bays—bays being added when required. They were invariably thatched, with the timbering, mainly of elm, which has been for centuries the dominant tree of the coastal plain—in contrast with the oak of the Weald clay, or the beech of the Downland chalk.

A second type of aisled barn, found widely over the south west area of the county, has aisles continued round both ends, and the barns are seldom of more than three bays. The result is a squarish building, measuring on average 30 feet in width by 45 feet in length. Like the long aisled barns, they seem almost invariably to have been thatched, but the continuation of the aisle round the ends made any extension virtually impossible. Both these types of aisled barn appear to date from the late 17th and 18th centuries, and it is in this period that they became standardised to meet the needs of increased corn production and larger farms. Both are rapidly decreasing in number since, of all forms of barn, the aisled is least adapted to modern needs and the cost of rethatching prohibitive.

A third kind of aisled barn has a much wider distribution over the western part of Sussex, extending into Hampshire and northwards into Surrey and is aisled on one side only. The advantage of a single aisle is that the eaves on the non-aisled side are high enough to admit the largest loaded wagon. These barns are usually of three bays and therefore smaller than the others. They are almost always attached to cattle byres or 'hovels' built at right-angles to the ends of the barn forming a sheltered enclosure or yard. They were principally hay barns associated with the growth of dairy farming, and the majority were built between the middle of the 18th and the middle

129 *Cross in Hand, post mill*

130 *'This mill was drawn on the 28th March 1797 from Regency Square to ye Dyke Road, Brighton, a distance of over two miles by 86 oxen ...'. Oxen were used extensively in Sussex for draught work, until well into this century.*

131 *A shepherd watering his flock at a dewpond. Man-made dewponds were the main source of drinking water for sheep on the chalk downs. Usually circular, they were lined with straw and puddled clay and they collected rainwater or condensed mist.*

132 *A Sussex trug*

of the 19th century. It is probable, however, that this arrangement of barn and byre has a very early ancestry.

Over the county as a whole the aisleless barn predominates. They do not vary much in plan, but there is plenty of scope for variation in size or materials. They range from relatively small medieval timber-framed barns with crownpost roof construction and covered with Horsham slab tile in parts of the Weald to the great flint and brick barns in the Downs. They can date, though only a few, from the late Middle Ages to the middle of the 19th century, when corn production in the county reached its peak. The unaisled barn is more adapted to conversion to other purposes; and a number have in fact been converted to houses.

Another development, which began in the 17th century and which became general in the 18th, was the construction of separately designed granaries for the safer storage of thrashed corn. These were relatively small buildings raised from the ground on mushroom shaped staddle stones, protecting the grain from rising damp and vermin. In earlier days, thrashed corn was more often stored on an upper floor in barns, or even in attic stores in the farmhouses; but with the growth of larger farms a specialised building became not only more desirable, but more feasible. Granaries were built not only for grain already thrashed, but for stacking unthrashed corn also.

XIV *Chichester. The City walls can be clearly seen in the foreground. The main roads meet at right angles at the cross and follow the Roman plan. The open space in the north-east corner is Priory Park containing the remains of the Norman Motte, and the Church of the Franciscan Friars. Beyond the walls at this point the Festival Theatre is just visible. In the foreground can be seen the Cathedral, the Bishop's Palace and the Deanery.*

XV *The town of Lewes can be seen spreading out from around the defensive mound of the castle. The wharves and warehouses along the River Ouse are in the foreground.*

XVI *Gatwick Airport, the second busiest international airport in the world with a capacity of dealing with some 25 million passengers a year.*

Later in the 19th century it was not unusual for hay to be stacked in this way and, towards the end of the century, cast iron staddles with supporting round or rectangular framework for the base of the rick were being used in the north of the county for this purpose. Although these granaries, like the barns, have little use today and are disappearing, the evidence of their existence remains in the staddle stones which can be seen lining the drives to dozens of farmhouses in the county. By the middle of the 19th century there must have been few farms in the corn growing areas without one or more granaries mostly built within the previous hundred years.

Another farm building, which from the late 18th century onwards became a characteristic structure on the larger farms, was the round-house and horse gin. In this a horse or ox walking round a central turning post transmitted power to a series of geared cog-wheels to drive whatever machinery could be attached within the barn. These round-houses provided shelter for the animals and mechanism, but were usually open at the sides. They were built against the barn, the shaft, geared to the turning post,

133 Hurdlemaking. When Downland sheep farming was at its height during the latter part of the 19th century and early part of the 20th century, there was a huge demand for wattle hurdles made from coppiced hazel. Many country people worked as woodland craftsmen making a wide variety of products, not only from hazel but also from other underwood such as chestnut and ash.

passing through the barn wall. Many more of these existed in the 19th century than was previously supposed, but with the development of steam power they became so rapidly obsolete, and were so unsuitable for adaptation to any other use, that very few have survived. For this reason we often fail to realise how important this form of power was in every aspect of rural economy in the past, whether on the farm, in the brickyards, or even for drawing water from a well. Water and wind power is perhaps better appreciated today than that of horse or ox.

The 1820s saw a hectic period of windmill construction. All available water-power had long been fully utilised, and steam power was not yet in sight. The rapid increase in population and corn production resulted in the exploitation of wind power to the fullest extent. Few villages would be out of sight of at least one or two, and most of these would have been built within Cobbett's lifetime. Within two miles of the centre of Hastings there were 16 windmills, and a number more

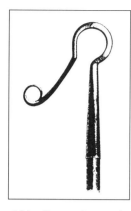

134 *Pyecombe crook*

135 *Smock mill, Shipley*

136 *Donkey   wheel,
Saddlescombe*

would have been visible from Castle Hill; within two miles of Brighton there were at least eight, with a dozen more visible from any of the hills in the vicinity. Not only were these new windmills a striking addition to the landscape, but they contrasted with the simply constructed post-mills of the earlier centuries. These new towers, or smock mills as they were called, in which only the cap or top storey, which carried the sails and driving shaft, turned to face the wind, could be very much higher and larger than the post-mills in which the whole structure pivoted on a central post. Their greater size, and the elaborate and delicate automatic devices with which they were fitted for turning the sails into the wind, or adjusting them to the changing wind velocity, represented a technical achievement comparable with the revolution in industrial techniques in the Midlands and the North.

Today only a few survive in ruin or semi-ruin. Of these, 11 have been restored. Those at Salvington, Oldlands near Ditchling, 'Jill' above Clayton are of the older post-mill type; the Cross in Hand and Argos mill (near Rotherfield) are post-mills mechanically turned by geared fantails running on a circular rail on the ground. The mills at Rottingdean and Chailey and the Kingsland mill at Shipley are wooden smock mills. Those at Patcham and Halnaker are brick tower mills, while the mill at Blatchington (above Hove) is built on a platform over the end of a barn. So there are preserved a few examples of something which a hundred years ago formed one of the most memorable features of the Sussex landscape.

Farm livestock was also the subject of development during this period. At the end of the 18th century John Ellman of Glynde was pioneering changes in the native sheep of the Sussex downs, the Southdown, which were to make them the finest quality meat sheep in the world, bearing wool of considerable value.

Cattle, mostly from the red Sussex breed, were still the primary draught animal at the turn of the century in the county. With the rise of population and the huge increase in the demand for meat, the rangy oxen were changed from plough animals to meat animals with the weight on their hindquarters. In Sussex, despite the increased use of horses on the land, draught oxen continued to be worked in some parts until very late indeed—the 1920s-1930s.

Underlying all the change over the last 300 years has been the steady increase in the scale of farming, in the size of farm units and in the amount of capital sunk in farm equipment. This has been more rapid in the last two decades than in any previous period. Perhaps one of the most significant recent developments has been the increasing size not merely of farms, but of fields by the destruction of the hedges and field divisions which the initial process of consolidation by enclosure in the 15th and 16th centuries had created. In some parts of Sussex—in the south-west region in particular—we may soon have a landscape more closely resembling, in everything except the buildings and the social and economic organisation underlying its use, that of the 13th-century open fields than at any time since the Middle Ages.

14

Victorian and Edwardian Sussex

Nationally the Victorian and Edwardian period was one of almost uninterrupted technological progress. Sussex is regarded as a backwater, bypassed by the developments of the Midlands and the North. This, however, is not quite true. There were no important industries located in Sussex, no new factories using new techniques and demanding an expanding class of industrial workers; yet many new developments were pioneered in the Brighton area.

137 *Brighton and the Chain Pier, c.1850, looking east from the edge of the Pool valley. In the 1980s the Sealife Centre would occupy the immediate foreground with the Palace Pier on the right and Brighton Marina was to extend into the sea from below the cliffs on the horizon.*

138 *Seahouses, Eastbourne, 1834. The village lay nearly a mile inland. The development of Eastbourne was almost entirely between 1850 and 1900. Of all the Sussex resorts it was the most completely Victorian in character, and has grown relatively slowly this century.*

Inside the Royal Pavilion, Nash had been among the first to use cast iron beams and columns, modelled decoratively and appropriately, not merely in the kitchen, but in principal state rooms such as the saloon and drawing room. The Antheum at Hove, built in 1831 as a great glass and metal dome, antedated, in the boldness of its design and its size, both the Crystal Palace and the Reading Room of the British Museum. It was unfortunate that it collapsed on the day before it was due to open, but even this tragic miscalculation provided data for the later and more successful ventures. The chain pier was a pioneer work and first demonstrated the possibility of a suspension system applied to tremendously increased forces of wind and wave. It was finally carried away in a storm in 1896 but this was nearly half a century after it had outlived its original purpose as the main terminus for the cross channel traffic service.

In the 1880s, the cable car suspended across Devil's Dyke and the cable lift up the steep northern escarpment of the Downs were at the time among the earliest experiments of their kind, although the visitor to the Dyke today will see nothing to indicate that they ever existed.

In 1883, the first railway in the world to be powered by electricity was built by Mr. Volk along the undercliff at Kemp Town: this still runs. In 1896 a unique railway was laid just above the low tide level. At high tide this carried passengers on a covered platform raised high above the waves. This novelty was nicknamed 'Daddy Longlegs': for five years until its dismantling at the beginning of the present century it entertained thousands of visitors.

Brighton, however, is not rural Sussex, and during the aftermath of the Napoleonic war the situation in the countryside was very different.

139 *Victorian farm labourers at Charlton on the Goodwood Estate in about 1890. Eighteen people were employed on this 600-acre tenanted farm. The farm now forms part of the estate home farm which totals over 3,000 acres and employs just seven people.*

140 *A royal house party at West Dean for Goodwood raceweek in 1899. As Prince of Wales, and later as King, Edward VII was a frequent guest of Mr. and Mrs. Willie James, the owners of West Dean Park. Mrs. James was a famous Edwardian hostess and her son Edward established the Edward James Foundation as a Charitable Educational Trust in 1964. The house became a college, where traditional arts and crafts and the conservation and restoration of antiques are taught.*

141 *Goodwood Racecourse during the late 19th century. Racing had been started by the third Duke of Richmond in 1801. The Grandstand seen here was built in 1830 by the fifth Duke and could accommodate 3,000 people. King Edward VII was a regular visitor to Goodwood and described the meeting as a 'garden party with racing tacked on'.*

Cobbett wrote his descriptions of Sussex at a time of general agricultural depression, created by falling prices and accompanied by widespread unemployment. A few years later these conditions reached their climax. In certain parts of the county there were outbreaks of violence, mostly rick-burning or window-breaking. At Rye the unpopular overseer of the parish poor, who was responsible for the payment of outdoor relief and controlled the local poorhouse, was conducted by a crowd of five hundred along the turnpike road, and deposited outside the confines of the parish. The people of the parish were then regaled with beer by the farmers whose sympathy was in many instances with the labourers. In these 'riots' which spread to Brede, then to Ringmer, and finally to the area round Horsham, little personal violence was shown. The demands of the labourers were, in fact, singularly moderate. At a packed meeting of nearly a thousand held in the parish church at Horsham demands were formulated for a wage of 2s. 6d. per day, and the lowering of rents and tithes. The High Sheriff for Sussex, in a letter to the Home Office, wrote: 'I should have found it quite impossible to have prevailed upon any person to serve as special constables—most of the tradespeople and many of the farmers considering the demands of the people but just and equitable.'

From Sussex the demonstrations spread into all the other southern counties. It was, as J.L. Hammond describes it in *The Village Labourer*, 'the last Labourer's Revolt'. The measures taken to repress them, and the punishments inflicted, were out of all proportion to the offences committed. Arson was then a capital offence and four men were condemned for rick-burning at the assizes at Horsham, between 1831 and 1834, and publicly executed in front of the gaol. They included George Wren, a workhouse orphan of 19, who was later proved to have been trying to put out the fire.

The distress and agitation of the 'thirties finally came to an end with the return of agricultural prosperity, brought about by the rise in the price of corn due to the steady pressure of population in the Midlands and the North. Richard Cobden, son of a Sussex yeoman farmer near Midhurst, for years led the agitation for the repeal of the Corn Laws by which the price of corn was maintained by taxes on imported grain. He was vindicated in the years immediately following the repeal in 1846. Farmers were not ruined by foreign competition; on the contrary, the later 'fifties and the 'sixties are often referred to as 'the golden age of English agriculture'. The rural population of Sussex increased steadily without creating any large measure of unemployment; by 1870 more land was under the plough than at any time before or after. About 1870, however, the tide began to turn again; cheaply produced corn from America, Poland and Russia forced down the price of English grain, and land went out of cultivation. The decline was greatest in those areas where land of marginal quality had been ploughed up; large tracts of the Weald consisted of land of this kind. And so, between 1870 and the outbreak of the First World War, the character of the Sussex landscape, particularly of the heavier clay and sandstone areas, was transformed from a checkerboard of fields whose colour changed from browns to green and gold with the seasons, to one of unvaried meadowland—from

142 *Cobden Memorial, Heyshott*

corn growing to pasture and milk production. The climax of this change was reached in 1932. Detailed field maps of several parishes which survive from the 16th century show that a far larger area was then under the plough than in 1932. This decline is reflected in the census figures; a great many parishes in the purely rural areas of Sussex had a much smaller population in 1931 than in 1871.

POPULATION COMPARISON

	1901	1991
Horsham	13,000	39,142
Chichester	10,000	24,400
Crawley	4,000	87,644
Worthing	25,000	100,305
Shoreham/Southwick	7,000	31,725
East Grinstead	6,000	22,086
Bognor Regis	13,000	55,772
Brighton	103,000	143,582
Eastbourne	44,000	81,395
Hastings	66,000	80,820
Hove	30,000	85,364
Lewes	11,000	15,376

Other changes began in the 1830s which were to have lasting consequences. In 1832 the first Reform Bill changed the traditional system of representation in Parliament, unaltered since the 13th century. Several of the Sussex boroughs, such as Winchelsea and Bramber, had declined into the worst kind of 'rotten borough', others had become 'pocket boroughs' in which the bulk of the properties, to which votes were traditionally attached, were owned by the local great family. Sir George Trevelyan describes the election of Charles James Fox, then aged 19, for whom the constituency of Midhurst was selected in 1768: 'The right of election rested in a few smallholdings on which no human being resided, distinguished among the pastures and the stubble that surrounded them by a large stone set up on end in the middle of each portion. These burbage tenures, as they were called, had all been bought up by a single proprietor, Viscount Montague [of Cowdray] who, when an election was in prospect, assigned a few of them to his servants, with instructions to nominate the members and then make back the property to their employer.'

By the Act of 1832 Bramber, East Grinstead, Seaford, Steyning and Winchelsea lost both their members: Arundel, Horsham, Midhurst and Rye were reduced to single member constituencies. Since then various Acts modified the parliamentary map of Sussex; new boroughs were created in Brighton, Hove and Eastbourne, and only Hastings of the 13 original Sussex boroughs still has, as a town, a representative in Parliament.

In 1834 the Poor Law Amendment Act altered the whole structure of the system which had been established in the reign of Elizabeth, by which each parish was responsible for the care of its own poor. Parishes varied greatly, but Commissions of Enquiry described appalling conditions in some of the parish workhouses in Sussex. At Shipley a small thatched cottage housed

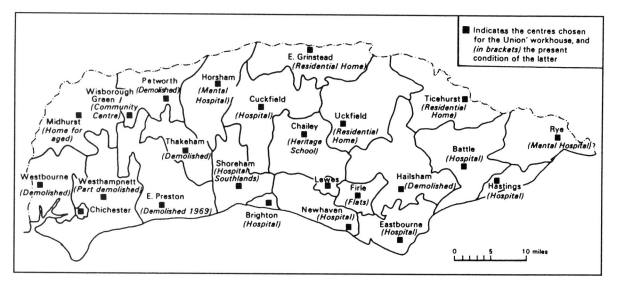

143   *Poor Law Unions*

144 *The courtyard of Sackville College, East Grinstead. The almshouses were founded by the second Earl of Dorset in 1609.*

up to twenty children, mostly orphans or illegitimate, verminous and half starved, sleeping on straw. Many such children were destined, as soon as they were old enough, to be 'apprenticed' to some cotton or woollen manufacturer in the north; by this kind of forced migration, the rural areas of Sussex supplied cheap labour for the industrial towns. In contrast, the workhouse at Easebourne near Midhurst, built through the initiative of the third Lord Egremont in 1798, served as a model for the rest of the country, with workrooms, handicraft instructors and nurses. Solid and well designed, it was built under an act of Parliament in 1782 (Gilbert's Act), which enabled parishes to combine for the maintenance of their poor. In this case 12 parishes co-operated and what was achieved at Easebourne had some influence on the form of the Act of 1834, in which the parish system was everywhere abandoned in favour of workhouses maintained by groups of parishes or 'Unions'. Under this Act 20 unions were formed and new work-houses were built in various parts of Sussex—bleak, barrack-like structures, mechanically efficient and, though perhaps preferable to the Shipleys, lacking the informality, and sometimes the humanity, of the converted cottage in the village, where at least there would be local ties and contacts. During the 1830s emigration was encouraged, notably from Petworth to Canada, funded largely by Lord Egremont. Since then there have been many changes and reforms: the Local Government Act of 1929 finally abolished the 'Work-house System' of 1834. Redundant and over-large country mansions of an earlier age, such as that of the Bartelott family at Stopham, have been converted into old people's homes—a final use which the original builders could hardly have foreseen.

145 *Village school, North Heath*

A third development which traces back to the 1830s lies in education—then the first grants were voted by Parliament to religious bodies to help in the building of schools in areas where there were none. Under this and subsequent legislation, culminating in the Education Act of 1870 by which primary education was made compulsory and universal, schools were built in practically every village in Sussex, two-thirds of them by the Church of England. Since then ideas of accommodation and class management have changed; buildings then erected are out of date; many, under the Education Act of 1944, have been closed, some converted into public halls, some to private houses, while others have been pulled down. They were, in fact, often too well and solidly built, and occasionally we must regret the loss of the small local school on the edge of a common, where the children of the village with their teacher had something of the quality of a happy family.

Canals and Railways

'Soon after quitting Billinghurst I crossed the river Arun, which has a canal running alongside of it. At this there are timber and coal yards, and kilns for lime. This appears to be a grand receiving and distributing place.' So writes Cobbett, in 1823. He is referring to the Wey-Arun canal, which had recently been completed, linking the Arun with the Thames. This canal connected places like Chichester, Littlehampton and Midhurst with the great network of canals which radiated from London to the Industrial North, to East Anglia and even to the West Country as far as Welshpool and Bristol. The burst of canal building, which eclipsed that of the turnpikes earlier, and even that of the railways later, was confined mainly to the years 1790-1815. By 1820 it had come to an end. It may seem surprising that most of our canals were built while we were at war with Napoleon. In fact the war acted as a stimulus, since the canals provided an alternative to the coastal shipping trade—until then the principal method for the transport of heavy and bulky goods and now subject to constant interference by French raiders. One of the Sussex canals—that from Rye to Hythe, skirting the north edge of the Romney marsh—was purely military. Designed to move men, artillery and equipment rapidly and within the coastal area, it also served as a line of defence against any invasion force. Another canal projected for military purposes, but in fact never built, was one which would have linked Portsmouth and Chatham, the

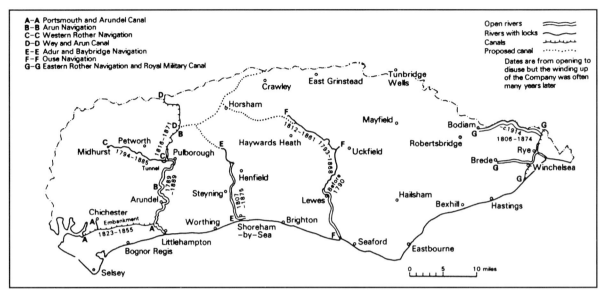

146 *Canals*

two great naval bases. Several alternative routes were considered, one of which, via Chichester and Arundel, would have followed the flat Weald clay through the centre of Sussex, via Horsham and Crawley, to link with the Medway above Tonbridge.

Although military considerations played their part, the main function of most of the Sussex canals was the improvement of agriculture, by the cheaper movement of heavy agricultural products and requisites. To quote Arthur Young: 'Though it be true that Sussex has hardly the shadow of anything that deserves the name of manufacture, yet the advantages which the County has received and is likely still further to gain from increasing her navigation will be very considerable. The principal productions of Sussex are, 1, corn; 2, timber, bark, charcoal; 3, chalk, lime, marl; 4, iron, marble, limestone; 5, cattle and sheep, hides and wool.' The barges were drawn by horses, but also carried sails for use when the wind was favourable. The first canals in Sussex were, strictly speaking, navigations. Their purpose was to make navigable the lower reaches of the rivers, which centuries of neglect had rendered useless as waterways for even small boats. This involved dredging, the removal of sandbars, and occasionally the shortening of the winding course of the river by joining meandering curves with a cut or 'true canal'. This phase did not normally involve the building of locks. The rivers in Sussex made navigable in this way were the Eastern Rother, the Ouse, the Adur, and the Arun.

The 'true canal' was an entirely new waterway, often climbing by means of locks over considerable watersheds, or by means of tunnels maintaining a level course beneath intervening ridges. The canal which linked the Arun Navigation to the Wey Navigation was one of this kind. It climbed by a series of 14 locks from Stopham near Pulborough to its highest point (in Sidney wood on the Surrey-Sussex border), where it just skirts the 150-foot contour. In places it curved along hillsides some 20 feet above the bottom of the valley.

Other enterprises were part navigation and part canal—such as the (western) Rother Valley Navigation and the extension of the Adur and Ouse navigations by a series of locks and cuttings further into the Weald. The Rother Navigation rose 86 feet from Stopham to Midhurst by a series of eight locks, at intervals of about one-and-a-half miles. A branch followed the little valley of the Haslingbourne to the south-east edge of Petworth built partly on an embankment; it crossed two or three small streams and included two locks.

Apart from the Wey-Arun and the Hythe military canal, the only other true canal in Sussex was the last to be built (1817-23). Its construction was due largely to the initiative and financial backing of the third Lord Egremont,

147 *An Edwardian view of the Hastings blacknet fishing shops. They were designed to maximise the small amount of space available for storing fishing nets. Traditionally a fishing port, Hastings had also become by the early 19th century a seaside resort. St Leonards to the west of Hastings was developed by James Burton as a fashionable resort during the late 1820s and early 1830s when it was visited by the young Princess Victoria.*

148 *The wharf at Newbridge on the Wey-Arun Canal, near Billingshurst. The warehouse in the photograph is one of the few surviving canal buildings and was described by Cobbett as 'having large timber and coal yards and kilns for lime, and appearing to be a grand receiving and distributing place'.*

149 *Eastbourne sea-front at the turn of the century: beaches crowded with holiday makers and bathing machines. Scenes such as this would have been common at all Sussex seaside resorts during the late Victorian and Edwardian periods.*

who had financed the Rother Navigation. It linked the Arun above Ford with Portsmouth. One reason for building it was the desire to provide employment during the depression which followed the end of the war with Napoleon. This canal, though it climbs to no great height and contains only four locks between Chichester Harbour (where it enters Sussex) and the Arun, is one of the most interesting in the south of England. It runs parallel to the coast, crossing at right-angles a number of small streams, the largest of these being the Aldingbourne Rife; here the canal runs for nearly half a mile along the top of an embankment some 10 feet above the surrounding meadows, the river running through a tunnel underneath the canal. The canal bed is dry today, and up to a few years ago a humped bridge stood to the south of Barnham in the middle of a farm-track, and, overgrown with a thicket and trees, it was apparently as purposeless as the bridge of Croyland.

The Portsmouth-Arun canal was, unlike the Rother Navigation, never a success. In no year did the tolls produce a reasonable return on the capital invested. By 1855 the canal was virtually abandoned, and in 1888 the Company was finally wound up. A small section at Birdham is still used as a safe anchorage for yacht and motor-boats, while the branch which led from Hunston to Chichester was acquired by the City Corporation, and in 1958 was taken over by the County Council to develop for leisure. The Chichester Canal Society now cares for it.

The other Sussex canal which would well repay preservation is the Military Canal at the other end of the county, traversing some of the loveliest and most remote countryside to be found anywhere in England.

The only tunnel in Sussex is that which shortened the Arun Navigation by cutting through the ridge at Hardham, along which the ancient line of Stane Street, the railway and the modern motor road run from Pulborough to Coldwaltham. This tunnel, and the lock to the south, was constructed to make it possible for barges to avoid the four-mile tidal loop at Greatham. Barges were propelled through the tunnel by the feet of the bargees who lay on their backs and pushed against the roof. Though the last barge passed through the tunnel in 1885, it was still navigable at the beginning of the century for a small skiff. Today not only are the entrances choked, but where the railway crosses the canal, concrete reinforcements completely block the canal, making any kind of reinstatement virtually impossible.

Of the various schemes put forward between 1800 and 1825 for a ship canal linking the Thames to Portsmouth, that of Cundy in 1824 was by far the most ambitious. To quote from the prospectus:

> This canal ... is intended to accommodate vessels of the largest dimensions when fully loaded so as to enable them to pass each other; for this purpose twenty-eight feet depth of water will be required and about a hundred and fifty feet in width, with about four locks, three hundred feet in length and sixty-four in depth up to the summit level.

150 *Original signal box, Hardham*

The line of the canal, leaving the Thames at Deptford, would have passed through the Mole gap at Dorking, and thence across the Weald to Arundel. At the highest point, approximately three hundred and eighty-two feet above sea level, it was designed to run through a cutting a hundred feet deep. Although nothing came of this and other schemes, they are some measure of the prodigious optimism and confidence of the engineers of the period. Within a little more than a decade these energies were to be transferred to the railways.

The decline of the canals was in fact almost as sudden and dramatic as that of the turnpikes, and for the same reason—the coming of the railways. In the 24 years between 1839 and 1863 the main lines in Sussex were completed.

151 *The Bluebell Railway at Horsted Keynes. The station is among the finest preserved in the country.*

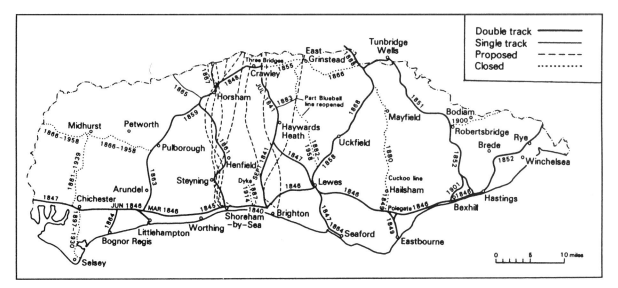

Of the secondary lines, the Mid-Sussex from Pulborough to Petersfield was opened in 1867, the section from Midhurst to Chichester in 1885; the Chichester to Selsey line in 1897. The 'Bluebell' line, as it came to be called, which linked the main line at East Grinstead with the main line just north of Lewes, was opened in 1882. The little railway that conveyed visitors from Victorian Brighton to the fun-fairs, cable railway and funicular on the Devil's Dyke was completed in 1887; it had a brief life of less than thirty years before being dismantled to serve in France during the First World War. After the war it was reinstated and closed finally in 1938. The Selsey line followed in 1935; the Chichester to Midhurst line was closed during the last war and the Pulborough to Petersfield section of the mid-Sussex railway was finally closed to both passenger and goods traffic in 1958. The 'Bluebell' line, after being closed by the Transport Commission in 1958, was reopened by private enterprise and is now a successful tourist attraction.

On the other hand, main lines such as the Brighton to London carry a weight and frequency of traffic undreamed of by their original promoters. When this line was first debated in 1863, eight rival schemes were put forward; five of these favoured the devious routes following the Adur valley through Steyning, or the Falmer valley to the east. That the final decision was the direct route through the Downs, necessitating one of the longest tunnels to be made at that time, indicates the foresight, as well as the supreme confidence, of the promoters; while the fact that the magnificent curved viaduct, which takes the Lewes line across the London road and into the hillside terminus at Brighton, can cope with such tremendously increased traffic is a testimony to the quality of early Victorian engineering.

It is, however, well to remember that these skills, as well as the labour force which enabled the railway development to be carried through so rapidly, were the result of the experience gained during the Regency period. Part of the labour then recruited for the equally difficult and occasionally more spectacular task of building the canals, was available for the building of railways. A train can go uphill, water cannot. The canal tunnels, viaducts and bridges all had to be planned with a greater nicety of judgement, and accuracy of measurement than their railway equivalents.

153 *Funicular, Devil's Dyke, 1890*

15

Twentieth-Century Sussex

Economic and Social Forces

History is concerned with the past, but one reason for studying history is the belief that it can provide clues to the future. During the 20th century—and particularly after the First World War—the conditions of life, the distribution and density of population, the character of the Sussex landscape, have changed more rapidly than in any previous period of similar duration. What is more, the tempo of change accelerated. These developments were due partly to migration into the area for residential or recreational purposes (a process which began in the Weald in the 16th century and on the coast in the 18th), partly to changes in agriculture and in the location of industry and increasingly to the technological revolution which was gathering momentum in the 1980s and 1990s.

In the opening years of the 20th century Sussex was dominated by the estates of Dukes and Earls—in the west they owned some 500,000 acres between them. The ravages of war and post-war development were to change the face of the county, with the influence of Gatwick Airport—the second busiest international airport in the world—the importance of light industry and proximity to London all playing vital rôles.

Despite this, in West Sussex by the end of the century the larger estates remained chiefly intact, and together with large farms across the county continued to provide rural employment although at a much reduced level. Only five per cent of the county's jobs were in agriculture and horticulture by 1994. In East Sussex 65 per cent of its 695 square miles was devoted to agriculture in 1993. This was the equivalent of 277,042 acres compared with the 1914 figure of 528,450 acres. In West Sussex the figure was 311,669 acres, compared with the 1914 figure of 400,285 acres. Forestry is also important—Sussex has some 154,375 acres of woodland; West Sussex is the second most densely-wooded county in the country.

As the century unfolded, school and road-building increased, hospitals were constructed, housing estates grew up and industrial estates mushroomed. Education, the health service and social services were all to experience revolutionary changes.

154 *Power station, Southwick, now demolished.*

The First World War

Before the First World War the population of Sussex was increasing steadily, but the rate of growth varied from area to area. The increase occurred along the coast or on the railway routes—most of the rural villages had declined in population since 1870. The development of road transport was having its effect on the countryside, leading to pepper-pot distribution of new houses, destroying the quality of one rural area after another. Some inland areas of West Sussex escaped this sprawling development, largely due to restrictive action taken by landowners. But this became increasingly less possible through the incidence of heavy death duties and the splitting up of some estates.

Call-up for war service depleted the county's workforce slowing development. Many Sussex men failed to return, dying in the trenches across the Channel. However, working people and women were to benefit from the changed attitudes after 1918; the first women were elected to West and East Sussex County Councils the following year. Sussex's traditional isolation was disappearing—the roads were improved; tar had first been used in West Sussex in 1902!

Between the Wars

Agriculture remained dominant. Encouraged by subsidies, farmers were to continue ploughing the downland from the 1940s through to the 1970s. Land untouched for 1,500 years was cultivated remorselessly. Conifer plantations, alien to the chalk landscape, were planted in tracts unsuitable for ploughland. The increase in agricultural production was made possible by mechanisation and the development of chemicals—the agricultural population, however, fell, declining from 22 per cent in West Sussex in 1881 to four per cent by the 1980s.

The threats to the countryside led to a growing public conscience and the formation of groups such as the Society of Sussex Downsmen. Planning was becoming vital, for urban and rural development, and West Sussex was the first county council to appoint a Planning Officer. By the closing years of the century concern for the natural environment was to be deeply felt by a majority of the population and measures to limit damage in place. The South Downs were created an Environmentally Sensitive Area (ESA), encouraging farmers and landowners, through Ministry of Agriculture grant aid, to farm sympathetically and maintain the landscape and chalk grassland. The foundation of the Sussex Downs Conservation Board in 1993 was to be the single most important development.

The inter-war period saw the expansion of horticulture. The largest mushroom-growing and processing plant in Europe operated near Pulborough, and the Worthing area and west along the coastal plain saw a steady increase in the size and number of glass-houses growing tomatoes and flowers.

Shanty towns, such as 'bungalow town' at Shoreham, grew up along the coast as people escaped the growing bustle of London. In East Sussex between Brighton and Newhaven plots for cheap housing were sold off. The railway improved communications and was responsible for the rapid development of East Grinstead, Burgess Hill and Haywards Heath. The growing number of elderly people migrating to the Sussex coast was to become a feature of the population profile.

The Second World War

In the Second World War airfields at Tangmere and Ford played a key rôle in the Battle of Britain and the county formed a major assembly point for the D-Day invasion. General Eisenhower, Supreme Commander of the Allied Forces, held his final briefing before D-Day in the *Ship Hotel*, Chichester.

Evacuee children doubled the school population, and West Sussex towns suffered air raids—they were on the flight path to London and an ideal place over which the enemy could jettison unused bombs. The worst incidents were at East Grinstead where a bomb fell on a crowded cinema and in Petworth where children died when their school was hit. Three thousand

bombs were dropped on Littlehampton alone. Defence works took place all along the Sussex coastline and the South Downs were pressed into food production, destroying traditional chalk downland used for grazing sheep.

155 RAF Tangmere played a significant rôle in the Battle of Britain and suffered severe damage in one raid, as seen in the photograph, from German dive bombers. Sussex coastal towns were in the front line from air attack. Bognor, Littlehampton and in particular Eastbourne were all to suffer, the latter becoming an evacuated area.

Post War

In the 20th century the population of West Sussex expanded considerably. From 166,000 in the 1891 census it grew to 700,000. Between 1930 and 1954 and again in the 1970s and 1980s West Sussex experienced the second largest population growth of any county in England. In East Sussex today 70 per cent of the residents live along the coast.

The county was chosen as an appropriate region for one of the proposed 'new towns'. Crawley changed from a small rural area in 1947 to a town of 90,000 people with associated businesses and industry. Each of the 10 neighbourhoods within the town had its own shopping and civic centre laid out to create something of the character and informality of a village green.

Gatwick Airport nearby had early beginnings in the 1930s when a private airstrip was created on a racecourse. By 1988 it had become the second

156 *The Body Shop processing plant and headquarters at Littlehampton,* above, *is now one of the world's major cosmetic companies.*

157 *The County Mall shopping centre,* below, *built in Crawley during the 1990s has over 100 shops together with eating facilities and children's crêche, and adjoining multi-storey carpark. It is the south east's largest covered mall.*

busiest international airport in the world, capable of dealing with 25 million passengers annually and providing 18,000 jobs. The Queen opened the second terminal that year. More than 100 airlines operate through it to worldwide destinations. The economic prosperity of Sussex was to be improved and sustained by the success of Crawley and its industrial base and Gatwick Airport with its flourishing international business.

The Port of Shoreham, established in 1760 and an important route to the continent during earlier times, is today the largest commercial port between Dover and Southampton. Principal traffic in the mid-1990s—mostly imports—included sea-dredged aggregates, oil and bitumen, stone and slag, scrap metal and cereals. Further along the coast, the Channel ferry port of Newhaven gave East Sussex a direct sea link with France; the port is also the home of a fishing fleet and attracts commercial shipping.

Extractive industries making use of the county's natural resources have also had a considerable effect on the character of the Sussex landscape. Sand, chalk, gravel and clay for brick and tile making developed in the 1940s, growing to 70 sites at its peak. This had reduced to 34 by the 1980s but production was greater. In the same decade oil was found and drilled beneath Singleton Hill north of Chichester.

Road improvement was vital to the viability of the economy. Improvements included the upgrading of the A24 Worthing-Horsham road, the A27 coastal road improvement, the expansion of the A23 to Brighton, the Brighton and Hove bypass and the building of the M23 to serve the huge growth areas of Crawley and Gatwick. The proximity of East Sussex to the motorway network to the north helped it develop a reputation as the financial services centre of the south east. In East Sussex, by the 1990s, 81 per cent of the working population was employed in service industries.

Horticulture, though less dominant than before, was still important in West Sussex where the development of new crops and techniques took place at the Institute of Horticultural Research at Littlehampton, the Horticultural Energy Research Establishment at Aldingbourne and ICI's Plant Protection Division whose headquarters are at Fernhurst.

Manufacturing industry provides a fifth of jobs, close to the national average, with 1970s employment in these industries growing rapidly in West Sussex against national trends. These were chiefly in pharmaceuticals (Beechams at Crawley and Worthing, Ciba-Geigy at Horsham and Scherings at Burgess Hill), electronics (Ericsson at Horsham and VG Scientific at East Grinstead) and light engineering such as refrigeration at LEC, Bognor Regis. Service industries were of growing importance as the century closed (Sun Alliance at Horsham, London and Edinburgh at Worthing and Citibank Life at Haywards Heath). The largest single concentration of industry is at Crawley where Duracell, Rediffusion, Canon, Thorn EMI and ROCC Computers have a base.

158 *Sussex University, main entrance*

West Sussex County Council was a leader in computerisation, the first to introduce a computer-controlled system in its libraries and the first to launch a computerised immunisation schedule for its children. The comprehensive system of secondary education was introduced to both counties in the 1960s and 1970s. In 1992 West Sussex was the top county in the first national league table of GCSE exam results. Numbers of pupils staying on for A levels were among the highest in the country. The national curriculum was introduced in all schools. New legislation removed part of the traditional local authority rôle in the provision of education, and local management enabled schools to manage their own budgets and programmes within the county support system. The University of Sussex opened at Falmer north of Brighton, to be joined by the University of Brighton in the 1990s, providing East Sussex with a seat of academic learning.

Tourism—widely forecast as the growth industry of the millennium— shifted away from the traditional seaside family holiday, forcing coastal towns to rethink their economic strategy. With its beautiful countryside and scenic heritage Sussex, however, remains in a good position to benefit from the industry.

East Sussex, particularly Brighton and Hastings, suffered high unemployment as the recession of the early 1990s had its effect, and qualified for European financial assistance. The need to dispel the old image of a seaside and retirement county and take full advantage of the proximity of the Channel Tunnel and European markets was becoming paramount as the century closed.

As privatisation gathered momentum as a political ideal during the 1980s and 1990s the local authorities which had been critical in shaping Sussex life for the previous 100 years were grappling with a changing rôle—becoming enablers rather than providers. The Local Government review of the 1990s resulted in the creation of a new unitary authority for Brighton and Hove and confirmed the preference of the people of the rest of Sussex for the established pattern of county, district and parish councils. Partnership between authorities and the private and voluntary sectors became the watchword for the new century.

Conserving the Heritage

Public attention was first drawn to the tremendous pressures being imposed on the Sussex environment during the 1920s, when in the absence of any planning control the Downs became increasingly under threat from speculative building. The development of Peacehaven was instrumental in the foundation of the Society of Sussex Downsmen in 1923. The Council for the Protection of Rural England, founded in 1926, also played a part in arguing the case for conservation in the wake of proposed urban development and new roads. Brighton Corporation, Eastbourne Corporation and the National Trust all bought sections of downland and coastline to prevent development. The Sussex landscape was by this time already a popular subject for writers such as Richard Jefferies, W.H. Hudson, Rudyard Kipling, Hilaire Belloc, and Arthur Beckett. Beckett's *Sussex County Magazine*, produced during the inter-war years, did much to record the traditional, but rapidly changing, rural life of the county.

Archaeology

However it is the post-war years, particularly the last thirty, that have seen the most activity to conserve the Sussex countryside and built heritage, as well as the development of major artistic and cultural projects. Many of the most significant developments have been through the initiative of private bodies and individuals. The preservation of the Roman Palace at Fishbourne, which could have been lost forever, is one of the most exciting archaeological discoveries to have taken place nationally in modern times. The site is owned by the Sussex Archaeological Society, founded in 1846, which also owns other important archaeological sites in the county, including the castle and Anne of Cleves House in Lewes, Michelham Priory, Marlipins Museum in Shoreham, the Long Man of Wilmington, and the Priest House at West Hoathly. Specialist archaeological advice in Sussex is provided by the County Archaeological Officers. Field work is now mainly undertaken by tendering archaeological field units, but historically much of this work has been carried out by the former Chichester District Unit, now Southern Archaeology (Chichester) Limited or South East Archaeological Services.

Local societies and special interest groups also play an important rôle in the archaeological field. In recent years industrial archaeology has attracted increasing public interest. This has tended to concentrate on the impact of the industrial revolution and the way new inventions, technology and techniques of production have changed the character of life over the last

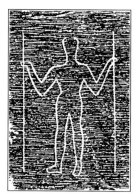

159 *The Long Man of Wilmington*

three centuries. Although essentially rural in character, Sussex has a rich industrial history revolving around the uses of its natural raw materials such as chalk, clay, iron ore and timber; as well as many buildings associated with industrial uses incorporating wind, water, power, transport and communications. Since its foundation in 1967 the Sussex Industrial Archaeology Society has done valuable work in the research and restoration of buildings, sites and machinery of the county's industrial history. The Amberley Museum was founded in the late 1970s by the Southern Industrial History Centre Trust. Located on the site of former chalk pits used to produce lime, the museum now has a wide range of exhibits covering the industrial heritage of the region. The Sussex Mills Group forms part of the Sussex Industrial Archaeology Society, and aims to promote the recording, preservation and restoration of the county's many mills.

160 *Nutley Windmill in 1970, now restored*

The growth of public interest in the recent industrial past is also well illustrated in the way in which the 'Bluebell Line' has been able to develop since its closure by British Railways in 1958 and its re-opening by enthusiasts. It has succeeded in recreating the character of the railway as it was during the first four decades of its existence. Another example can be taken from the county's water transport heritage. Since its formation in 1970, the Wey & Arun Canal Trust has been successful in restoring six locks and 16 bridges and clearing approximately seven miles of canal. The Trust's ultimate objective is to reopen 'London's lost route to the sea', and make it possible again to travel by boat from Arundel, through the heart of the Weald, to the Thames.

Natural History, Landscape and Buildings

Archaeology, however, illustrates but one aspect of conservation. There are other facets which affect our day-to-day response to the past and our sense of historic continuity—natural history, landscape and buildings. The Sussex Wildlife Trust was founded in 1961 and is devoted to the conservation of the natural heritage of Sussex. It is now the most influential voluntary organisation involved with nature conservation in the county. Based at the Woods Mill Countryside Centre, near Henfield, the Trust has 7,000 members and owns or manages more than 800 hectares of land in 37 separate nature reserves. These include important sites such as the ancient woodland of the Mens, north of Petworth; Amberley Wildbrooks and the Pevensey Levels. In addition, Sussex has five national nature reserves—Lullington Heath, Mount Caburn, Castle Hill and Pevensey Levels in East Sussex and Kingley Vale in West Sussex.

The Wildfowl and Wetlands Trust's reserve at Arundel was established in 1976 on land leased from the Duke of Norfolk which had once been water meadows. A branch of the organisation founded by Sir Peter Scott in 1946 at Slimbridge in Gloucestershire, it uses the same unique formula of combining a large collection of tame ducks, geese and swans from all over the world with areas set aside for wild fowl. The reserve has expanded its facilities over the years and contributed to the public's appreciation of the importance of wetlands in a highly imaginative and entertaining way. During the last few

years another bird and wildlife reserve has been opened in the Arun Valley by the Royal Society for the Protection of Birds at Pulborough.

Ashdown Forest is important in the context of countryside conservation. Located in the north of the county, this once royal hunting forest was surrounded by a pale fence during the Middle Ages to enclose deer. A series of Acts of Parliament towards the end of the 19th century established a Board of Conservators to protect commoners' rights and preserve the Forest. In 1988 it was purchased by East Sussex County Council which established the Ashdown Forest Trust to manage the Forest through the Board of Conservators.

Chichester Harbour is managed by Chichester Harbour Conservancy. Extending to some 11 square miles of inter-tidal waters and 17 miles of navigable channels, this major Area of Outstanding Natural Beauty now offers probably the best sailing for small boats in the country. The High Weald and the South Downs are the two other A.O.N.B.s covering Sussex.

The National Trust is responsible for maintaining a number of Sussex properties, gardens, countryside, coastline and downland. These include Petworth House, Batemans and Bodiam Castle, and the magnificent gardens of Nymans, Sheffield Park and Wakehurst Place, although the latter are administered by the Royal Botanic Gardens at Kew. The Trust celebrated its centenary in 1995 and its rôle played at either end of this period is worthy of note. The Alfriston Clergy House was the first building to be purchased by the Trust, for £10 in 1896. In 1995 the restoration of Uppark, South Harting was completed after its destruction by fire in 1989. At an estimated cost of £20 million, it has been the largest conservation project undertaken by the Trust and one of major national importance. In the same year the Trust bought Devil's Dyke and Saddlescombe Farm, north of Brighton, protecting an important stretch of downland landscape and a traditional farm with a remarkable range of unspoilt farm buildings. A landscape feature of the central Weald is its many beautiful gardens. These include Leonards Lee, High Beeches and Borde Hill in addition to those administered by the National Trust.

To be effective, however, the conservation of buildings and landscape must be the concern of local authorities and particularly important have been the post-war Town and Country Planning Acts which have given increasing powers of action, enabling the listing of buildings and the designation of entire areas or streets in a town or village as conservation areas. The Countryside Act of 1968 enabled local authorities to establish Country Parks and Amenity Areas of various kinds. There are now eight Country Parks in Sussex ranging from the Seven Sisters in the charming and unspoilt Cuckmere Valley to Buchan Country Park, near Crawley.

Since first opening to the public in 1970, the Weald and Downland Open Air Museum at Singleton has done much to create awareness of the built environment of South East England. The museum, which is also a country park, has re-erected to date some 40 traditional buildings of the countryside and village that would otherwise have been destroyed. The museum holds an important research library and undertakes training in the field of building

164 *The medieval shop from Horsham,* above, *is now reconstructed at the Weald and Downland Open Air Museum, Singleton, but its fate prior to its removal to the museum was typical of many buildings in West Sussex town centres. The structure from Middle Street was a timber-framed double-jettied building containing two shops. Following numerous changes over the years, it was finally threatened by demolition,* below, *with the development of Horsham town centre in the 1960s. It was dismantled and reconstructed at the museum in its original form: its site is now occupied by ironmongers Robert Dyas and the street is pedestrianised.*

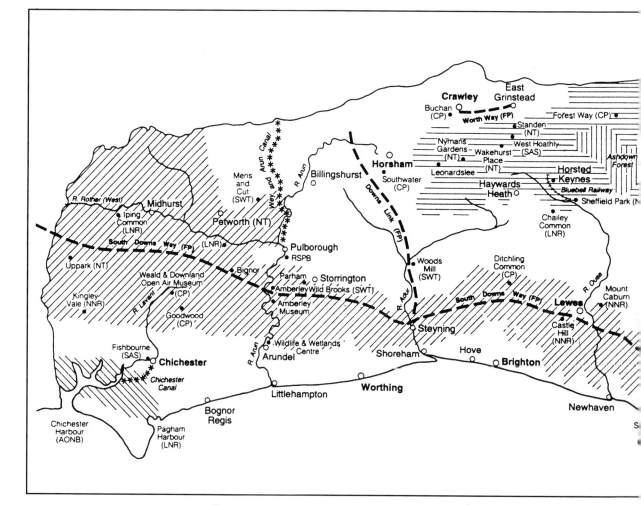

165 *Heritage and Con-*
servation

conservation, as well as supplying traditional building materials. The work
of volunteers and voluntary organisations in all aspects of conservation
work is vital. The Wealden Buildings Study Group is a good example of
dedicated enthusiasts recording timber-framed buildings. The Federation of
Sussex Amenity Societies has shown how a local group can influence development and help co-operation between the parties involved. Founded in 1967,
the Federation has over 100 member societies representing some 50,000
Sussex people.

Literature, Culture and Sport

It is impossible to mention all the distinguished people with literary or
artistic links with Sussex but most noteworthy are Hilaire Belloc who lived
at Slindon and then for much of his life at Shipley; William Blake who lived
at Felpham and was tried for sedition, and acquitted, at Chichester in 1804;
Rudyard Kipling who lived much of his life in East Sussex, firstly at

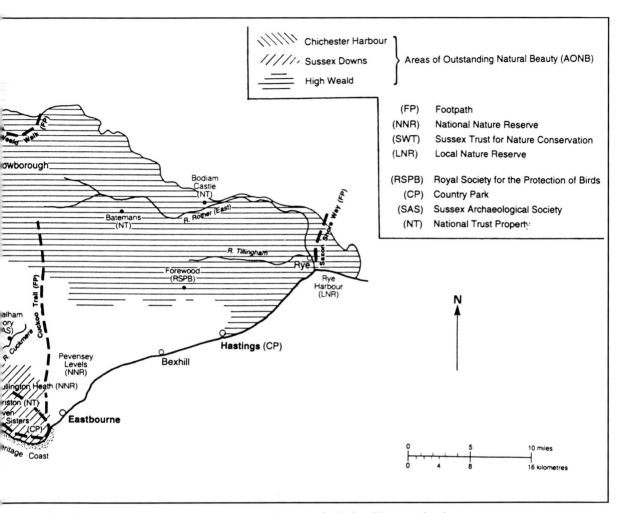

Rottingdean and then at Batemans, near Burwash; John Keats who began to write *The Eve of St Agnes* whilst visiting Chichester; Eric Gill who has connections with both Chichester and Ditchling; Shelley, who was born at Field Place, Warnham, near Horsham; J.M.W. Turner, who was a regular visitor to Petworth House where he painted his famous pictures of the Park, and Vanessa Bell who lived at Charleston Farmhouse, near Berwick, which was a retreat and meeting place of the 'Bloomsbury set'.

Two major cultural projects have received international acclaim. Glyndebourne, opened by John Christie in 1934, celebrated the opening of a new opera house in 1994. Chichester Festival Theatre, founded in 1959 by Leslie Evershed-Martin and opened in 1962, is famed for its hexagonal stage and has hosted a galaxy of theatrical stars over the last 30 years.

Changes in town centre design and shopping habits have had an effect on the environment and social behaviour. Pedestrian shopping precincts can be found in many main towns, but retailers have in recent years faced growing competition from out of town superstores.

166 *Chichester Festival Theatre has maintained an international reputation since its first season in 1962. Founded by Leslie Evershed-Martin, the theatre was designed by the architects Powell and Moya, who broke with tradition by designing a hexagonal stage.*

167 *The Wildfowl and Wetlands Centre at Arundel* (above left).

168 *The new Opera House at Glyndebourne opened in 1994* (above right).

Sussex has important sporting connections. The first reference to a game of cricket being played was in 1622 at Boxgrove Priory. Sussex men played an influential part in the development of the game over the next two centuries, notably the second Duke of Richmond and the Lillywhite family, one of whom captained the England team in the first test match against Australia. Founded in 1873, Sussex has yet to win the county championship. Two other games have strong Sussex associations. Every Good Friday Tinsley Green, near Crawley, hosts the Sussex marble championships and stoolball, a Sussex game similar to cricket, but traditionally played by women, still takes place.

As the dawn of the 21st century rapidly approaches, the balance between conservation and destruction has, with the exception perhaps of the influence of road building, swung towards conservation, reflecting the desire of Sussex people to protect their county heritage. This is a trend wholly in tune with the wishes of the author of this book, Roy Armstrong. If the economics of conserving heritage can be made to work over the forthcoming years—and this is by no means certain—then the struggles of all those concerned at the rapid pace of destruction will not have been in vain.

Bibliography

Publications devoted to the history of Sussex are numerous. We include below a selective list, including those which Dr. Armstrong and the editors of this edition have found most helpful:

Archives in the County Record Offices at Lewes and Chichester and the Sussex Archaeological Society, Lewes

The Sussex Records Society

The Burrell Collection

Cartwright and Dallaway's *History of the Western Division of the County*, published in four volumes between 1815 and 1832

The Victoria County History

Curwen, E.C., *Sussex* (County Archaeologies series)

Nairn and Pevsner, *The Buildings of England, Sussex* (Penguin, 1965)

Stanford, Thomas, *Sussex in the Great Civil War*

Young, Rev. Arthur, *General View of the Agriculture of the County of Sussex*

Mawer, A., Stenton, F.M., Glover, J.E.B., *The Place Names of Sussex*

Lucas, E.V., *Highways and Byways in Sussex* (1904)

Meynell, E., *Sussex* (Robert Hale, 1947)

Sussex County Magazine (1926-1956)

'Chichester Papers', edited by F.W. Steer

Robinson, M., *A Southdown Farm in the Sixties* (1938)

Roundell, R.A.E., *Cowdray House*

Straker, E., *Wealden Iron* (1931)

Kenyon, G.H., *The Glass Industry of the Weald*

Mason, R.T., *Framed Buildings of the Weald*

Vine, P.A.L., *London's Lost Route to the Sea* (the history of the Wey and Arun Canal)

Jessup, R. and F., *The Cinque Ports*

Shore, H.N., *Smuggling Days and Smuggling Ways*

Hadfield, C., *The Canals of South and South East England*

Marshall, C.D.F., *A History of the Southern Railway*

Cobbett's Rural Rides

Defoe, D., *A Tour Through the Whole Island of Great Britain 1724-6*

The Journeys of Celia Fiennes (*c.*1685-1702) edited by C. Morris

Brandon, P., *The Sussex Landscape* (Hodder and Stoughton, 1974); *The South Saxons* (Phillimore, 1979)

Brent, C., *Historic Lewes and its buildings* (Lewes Town Council Official Guide)

Brunnarius, M., *Windmills of Sussex* (Phillimore, 1979)

Clifton-Taylor, A., *Chichester* (B.B.C., 1984)

Down, A., *Roman Chichester* (Phillimore, 1988)

Drewett, P., Rudling, D., Gardiner, M., *The South-East to A.D. 1000* (Longmans, 1988)

Elleray, D.R., *Eastbourne* (Phillimore, 1978); *Hastings* (Phillimore, 1979); *Worthing* (Phillimore, 1972)

Garland, P., *Angels in the Sussex Air* (Sinclair-Stevenson, 1995)

Godfrey, J., Leslie, K., Zeuner, D., *West Sussex County Council—The First Hundred Years* (1988)

George, M., *The South Downs* (Pavilion Books, 1992)

Gray, J., *Victorian and Edwardian Sussex* (Batsford, 1973)

Guy, J., *Castles in Sussex* (Phillimore, 1984)

Harris, R., *Weald and Downland Open Air Museum Guidebook*

Hobbs, M., *Chichester Cathedral* (Phillimore, 1995)

Morris, J., *Domesday Book—Sussex* (Phillimore, 1976)

Pailthorpe, R., Serraillier, I., *Goodwood Country in old photographs* (Alan Sutton, 1987)

Pailthorpe, R., McGowan, I., *Chichester—A contemporary view* (John Wiley, 1994)

Pailthorpe, R., Payne, S., *Barclay Wills' The Downland Shepherds* (Alan Sutton, 1989)

Porter, V., *Southdown Sheep* (Weald and Downland Open Air Museum, 1991); *Village Parliaments* (Phillimore, 1994)

Poplett, R., *Peacehaven: A Pictorial History* (Phillimore, 1993)

Serraillier, I., *All Change at Singleton* (Phillimore, 1979)

Sorrell, A., *British Castles* (Batsford, 1973)

Sussex Environment, Landscape and Society (Alan Sutton, 1983)

Vigar, J., *The Lost Villages of Sussex* (Dovecote Press, 1994)

Wey and Arun Canal Trust, *Restoring London's lost route to the sea*

Trust for Wessex Archaeology Ltd., *Westhampnett* (1992)

Young, G., *A History of Bognor Regis* (Phillimore, 1983)

West Sussex County Council brochure, *Archaeology in West Sussex*

East Sussex and West Sussex County Guidebooks

Chichester District Archaeology Unit, annual reports

Field Archaeology Unit newletters (South Eastern Archaeological Services)

Guide and map to Ashdown Forest

Index